LEADERSHIP

COMPETENCIES THAT ENABLE RESULTS

KEN,

BEST OF LUCK IN LEADING

AS A COACH!

June '14

A Guide to Coaching Leaders to Lead as Coaches

LEADERSHIP
COMPETENCIES THAT ENABLE RESULTS

BOOK
1

of the
SCOPE of Leadership Book Series

MIKE HAWKINS
Award-Winning Author of
Activating Your Ambition: A Guide to Coaching the
Best Out of Yourself and Others

Brown Books Publishing Group
Dallas, Texas

The SCOPE of Leadership Book Series
A Guide to Coaching Leaders to Lead as Coaches
Leadership Competencies That Enable Results

Brown Books Publishing Group
16250 Knoll Trail Drive, Suite 205
Dallas, Texas 75248
www.BrownBooks.com
(972) 381-0009

A New Era in Publishing™

ISBN 978-1-61254-098-6
LCCN 2013930730

Printed in the United States
10 9 8 7 6 5 4 3 2 1

For more information or to contact the author, please go to
www.ScopeOfLeadership.com
www.AlpineLink.com

ABOUT THIS SERIES

Welcome to the SCOPE of Leadership book series. The six books in this series are designed to build your knowledge of the thirty-eight competencies of great leaders who lead as coaches. These books provide the insights and principles great leaders as coaches use to practice great leadership—the ability to achieve a desired result through the influence of people who follow and perform by choice.

By reading the SCOPE of Leadership book series, you will learn how to set the example you expect others to follow. You will learn how to coach and develop others, build trust and high-performance teams, and foster collaboration and innovation. You will understand what it takes to motivate and inspire others and discover how to impart ownership and stimulate engagement. You will learn how to develop engaging presentations and speak with confidence. You will understand how to craft win-win partnerships and manage conflict. Most importantly, you will learn how to shape organizational culture, operate with excellence, and deliver exceptional results.

The SCOPE of Leadership is for anyone who aspires to be a great leader. It is for business professionals who want to advance in their career as well as community leaders who want to make a positive impact on society. It is for parents and grandparents who want to be better examples to their children and raise them to be great leaders. It is for athletic coaches who want to help athletes become their best. It is for teachers, principals, church leaders, and others in positions of influence who aspire to influence people positively in order to reach a desired result.

CONTENTS

FIGURES

TABLES

ACKNOWLEDGMENTS

I thank my wife, Elizabeth, and my children, Allison, Angela, Emily, Corbin, and Mitchell, for their support and patience while I worked incessantly on developing and refining the content for this book series. For over eight years they were patient and understanding of the many family meals, conversations, and gatherings that I missed. I am grateful to have a loving family who supports and encourages me.

I thank my business partners who were instrumental in initially helping me establish Alpine Link's coaching and consulting practice: Amie Lawrence, Amy Hardin, Byron Swezy, Chip Toth, Chris Klinvex, Colleen Francis, Colleen Stanley, Jake Appelman, Jennifer Jones, Leslie Martin, Linda Davis, Mark Bodnarczuk, Mark Hooey, Matt Martin, Merit Gest, Mike Armour, Mike Danchak, Paul Hollrah, Rick Davis, Ron Magnus, and Tom Alafat.

I thank my editor, Daniel Millwee, who worked diligently to keep me focused on the main points of my message. His efforts made the SCOPE of Leadership book series succinct and straightforward to read. I also thank the rest of the staff at Brown Books Publishing Group, including Milli Brown, Cathy Williams, Cindy Birne, Danny Whitworth, Janet Harris, Jessica Burnham, Josh Masterson, Lucia Retta, and Omar Mediano for their help in making this series possible.

I thank you, the reader, for being interested in my work on leadership. It is you whom I envisioned as I spent thousands of hours putting this series together. I sincerely hope and pray that you find these books a worthy investment of your time. My goal is that they enable you to develop a coaching approach to leadership and become a great leader.

Most importantly, I thank my clients, in particular those in the early years of my consulting and coaching work. If it weren't for your engagement of my firm and trust in our Alpine Link team, I would not have had the opportunity to learn so much. You not only hired me and my partners but also allowed us to become your partners. It was through involvement with you and your organizations that I sharpened my understanding of leadership. It was through our work together that we gained deeper insights into the art and science of leadership. I am honored to be called your coach, advisor, trainer, and partner.

To all of you I am deeply indebted: Al Duff, Al Klein, Alan Deane, Alisa Marinelli, Alva Purvis, Alwyn Welch, Amit Balasubramanian, Anand Revashetti, Andy Morra, Andy Welsh, Assaf Litai, Atul Srivastava, Bari Abdul, Barry McPherson, Bill Dismuke, Bill McAlister, Bobby Hernandez, Brad Hargrave, Brent Remai, Brett Golden, Brett Larson, Brett Neilson, Brian Crowe, Brian Foster, Brian Longoria, Brian Myers, Brian Wray, Bruce Parelskin, Carl Spetzler, Charles Graft, Charlie Simpson, Chris Carter, Chris Geib, Chris Kennebeck, Chris Klinvex, Chris Noonan, Chris Stone, Christine Durham, Christopher Bray, Cindy Luoma, Clark Ellis, Clark Hulbert, Clark McDaniel, Cory Bushong, Craig Fellman, Craig Olson, Craig Parrish, Craig Wiseman, Dan McAllin, Danielle Fournier, Darrell Christian, Darrell Rodenbaugh, Darren Albert, Darrin Garlish, Dave Borger, Dave Dickison, Dave Finley, Dave Tripier, David Barker, David DeMartino, David Fishman, David Jackson, David Pearson, David Ries, David Roberts, David Walsh, Dennis Daniell, Dennis Omanoff, Devin Redmond, Dick Williams, Dillan Micus, Don Sather, Doug Hartley, Doug Wride, Ed Plucker, Eric Appel, Eric Launder, Erin Malone, Fernando Quintero, Fiaaz Walji, Francie Coulter, Frank Masi, Gary Davis, Gene Hodges, Gene Postma, Gerry Donnelly, Gordon Stout, Greg Carlson,

Greg Hampton, Greg Norwick, Greg Olek, Gregor McCole, Guy Fernandez, Haroon Fakiri, Harry Clarke, Jack Sebbag, Jack Taylor, James McGinley, James Pleasant, Jason Blevins, Jason Grier, Javed Hasan, J. D. Johnson, Jean-Pierre Bardet, Jeff Davidson, Jeff Henke, Jeff Pray, Jeff Ramsey, Jeff Tomlin, Jeff True, Jeffrey Moore, Jerry Allen, Jim Hamilton, Jim Lang, Jim Lewandowski, Jim McGinley, Jim Sargent, Jim Ulrich, Jim Vilbert, Jim Wilkerson, Joe Bob Baggett, Joe Telafici, Joe Yanda, John Bordwine, John Castaldi, John Davern, John Lichty, John McMahon, John Pinelli, John Thode, John Tredennick, Jon Lloyd, Joshua Martin, Kate Fitzpatrick, Kate Patterson, Katrina Warburton, Keith Weatherford, Ken McCray, Ken Webb, Kenton Sieckman, Kevin Campbell, Kevin Klinvex, Kevin Osterling, Larry Gescher, Lee Marshall, Leo Cole, Leslie Bertha, Lianne Caetano, Lorenzo Masi, Marcio Mello, Mark Bridgers, Mark Neely, Mark Scarmozzino, Mark Small, Mark Swanson, Mark Ziells, Matt O'Connell, May Yip, Michael Alterman, Michael Bolton, Michael Sgroe, Michael Waters, Mike Carpenter, Mike McParlan, Mike Sweet, Milo Riverso, Mindy Watrous, Nathan Mosley, Nick Artukovic, Paresh Mohanty, Pat Watson, Paul Hemson, Paul Noyd, Paul Wahlen, Paulette McLean, Pedro Gutierrez, Pete Knipe, Pete Lyons, Peter Braun, Phil SanDiego, Philip Bresnahan, Philip Nathan, Pravat Lall, Press Theriot, Rafael Alvarez, Ramon Peypoch, Ray Mussato, Reema Shown, Rick Charles, Rick Jackson, Robert Dyer, Robyn Cody, Rod Fisher, Ron Clanton, Rose Ranker, Ross Ferrin, Rudy Schmidt, Sajeena Warrier, Salvatore Cangialosi, Samir Eid, Scott Perian, Scott Price, Sean Slaton, Shailaja Shankar, Shari Ahlberg, Stacey Conner, Stephen Baker, Stephen Banbury, Steve Behrens, Steve Elliott, Steve Miller, Steve Petracca, Stu Rothenberger, Susan Brown, Susan Quam, Tenice Wehmeyer, Thevi Sundaralingam, Tim Darnell, Tim Morris, Tim Turner, T. J. Gill, Todd Gebhart, Todd Lowe, Tom Coakley, Tom Gibb, Tom Knight, Tracy Balent-Hamrac, Troy Craft, Troy Robinson, Twilla Case, Uy Huynh, Vito Ippolito, and William Morris.

INTRODUCTION

When I put the finishing touches on the SCOPE of Leadership book series, I couldn't help but reflect for a moment. My goal in writing the SCOPE of Leadership was to give you the most important and practical insights I've learned from my experience as an executive coach, management consultant, and leader. I wanted to provide you with the insight and motivation you need to become a great leader, whether in the workplace, community, or home. As the reader, you will be the judge, but I believe I accomplished my goal.

I've included the most popular content from my leadership training programs, the best practices from my professional coaching experience, and many lessons I've learned throughout my career. I've also included fascinating new insights from emerging behavioral science about how the brain works, how people behave in groups, and how people become motivated. I've incorporated human physiology considerations that impact leadership performance, elements of strategic thinking, and tactical principles that deliver operational excellence. I've included the essential management and leadership competencies required to be a great leader.

You will find that the SCOPE of Leadership is not a typical leadership resource based on management surveys or interviews of great leadership icons. It is not a documentary of a leader of a meteorically fast-growing company or someone popularized by the media, nor is it based on a historical analysis of past leaders or organizations. It is not a perspective from sitting in the ivory tower or the executive observation deck, nor one based on delusions of correlation between a perceived leadership behavior and unrelated result.

Rather, the perspectives on which the SCOPE of Leadership book series is based came from hands-on experience in a variety of roles not typical of most people's careers. They came from holding leadership positions in one of the world's largest companies as well as in one of the fastest-growing companies of all time, running several small businesses of my own, and serving on the board of several nonprofit charities. They came from my experience as a management consultant and executive coach. They also include an undeniable contribution from the analytical abilities I developed early in my career as an engineer.

My experience has given me the overarching perspective that people in positions of influence either enable or disable their organization's performance. Regardless of market conditions, the industry, or the people on their team, most achievements as well as most problems are rooted in leadership. An organization's performance is largely a result of the decisions, attitudes, and behaviors of people in positions of influence.

The SCOPE of Leadership focuses on the primary attitudes and behaviors I've found to be at the core of both achievement and failure. They are the mindsets and skills I've found to be consistently embodied by great leaders and missing in underperforming ones.

These attitudes and behaviors are the basis of the SCOPE of Leadership framework, which gives this book series a logical structure and straightforward approach to leadership. It turns the intangible nature of leadership into a tangible form—a roadmap that methodically guides you in learning and applying the leadership competencies of great leaders, with an emphasis on the competencies needed to lead as a coach. It puts the *why*, *what*, and *how* of leadership into an understandable context. This framework is unique in that it provides the detail needed to go from knowing how to be a great leader to putting your knowledge into practice and developing a coaching approach to leadership.

Part of my motivation to write the SCOPE of Leadership book series was to debunk popularized leader role models and emerging societal norms. It was also my intent to help people confront the natural human tendency to take the path of least resistance, which often steers people in a direction at odds with great leadership.

Our world is in a leadership crisis. Our businesses, communities, and families need people willing to take responsibility instead of avoiding it. We need leaders who are willing to put the best interests of their employees and constituents ahead of their own and who are willing to coach and develop the next generation of leaders.

An organization can be in a position of having great products, being part of a growth industry, having a large base of satisfied customers, and being highly profitable, but if it lacks a pipeline of great leaders, its future is bleak. Sustainable performance requires the continuous development of great leaders. It is the quality of leadership that ultimately enables or constrains an organization's performance and competitive position. That is the reason I believe the greatest threat to most organizations is not from the outside but from the inside.

Part of the problem is that leadership development is often reserved for senior executives rather than for emerging leaders and highly influential employees. Organizations too often think of leadership in terms of positions rather than in terms of influence and potential. Leadership isn't about people's titles but about what they do. For organizations to reach and maintain peak performance, they need leadership competence in positions at all levels—not just in the senior management team.

Another part of the leadership problem is that organizations focus managers on managing rather than leading. Many managers become managers because they were top performers in the domain of their profession. They were promoted from their individual contributor positions and never taught how to lead effectively and work through their people. As a result, they rely on crude management skills and their domain skills. They see their management role as a higher-level domain role. Hence organizations have many managers but few leaders.

The SCOPE of Leadership book series is written to help people in a position of influence and managers at all levels become great leaders. It is organized into six books that guide you in learning, understanding, and applying the principles of great leadership. This first book is an introduction that answers the most frequent questions I encounter about leadership. It provides the *what* and *why* of leadership. It also provides a comprehensive assessment that helps you identify where to focus your leadership development.

The remaining five books describe the thirty-eight competencies I've consistently found in great leaders. These books provide the *how* of leadership. They describe the enabling attributes and details of what you need to know and do to develop each competency. These books provide instructions, examples, models, and checklists that will guide you in exactly what you need to do to be a great leader.

As you read the SCOPE of Leadership, my intent is that you will be able to put the material into immediate application. You will be able to use it in your staff meetings, customer presentations, employee appraisals, supplier negotiations, and every other value-adding aspect of your responsibility. I suggest you grab a highlighter and pen. I think you will find yourself scribbling notes in the margins, dog-earing the pages, and making this book look like a well-used repair manual. These books are written to be an engaging first reading as well as a reference that you will come back to again and again. You might think of this book series as your leadership playbook, or if you tend to forget what you read, your leadership amnesia kit.

There is an ancient proverb that says, "When the student is ready, the teacher will appear." I hope you are ready and will accept my teaching. With so much to do and so little time to do it in, learning and development have fallen off the priority list for many people. But there is also so much to learn! If you are ready to learn, I believe you will find this book series to be a great resource.

I implore you to get off the treadmill of *busyness as usual* and take time to invest in yourself. When you do, you will receive a return that will more than offset your investment. You will be able to accomplish a great deal more in less time than you do now, perhaps more than you ever thought possible.

I hope and pray that the SCOPE of Leadership is the catalyst you need to become a great leader. Our families, communities, associations, organizations, and businesses need your leadership.

Mike Hawkins

CHAPTER ONE

THE NEED TO LEAD

The bottom line is down where it belongs—at the bottom. Far above it in importance are the infinite number of events that produce the profit or loss.

—Paul Hawken

For good reason there are so many schools, books, seminars, executive coaches, trainers, and human resource professionals focused on leadership. Study after study, year after year, finds that an organization's leadership is the most important characteristic impacting organizational performance. So with all the resources focused on leadership, you might logically conclude that great leadership is the norm in our society. Unfortunately, you'd be wrong. Despite the importance of leadership and investment in leadership development, studies also find that the quality of leadership continues to fall and set new lows. The gap between the characteristics leaders need in order to achieve high levels of performance and the characteristics leaders actually possess continues to grow.

Citizen polls reveal that over two-thirds of the public lacks confidence in government leaders. Over two-thirds of the public lacks confidence in public schools. Employee surveys consistently find that over half of employees consider their bosses to be below-average leaders. More shockingly, citizen polls and employee surveys alike often find even lower approval ratings, with many coming in as low as an abysmal 10 percent. Polls also find that nearly three-fourths of people think corporate corruption has increased in recent years, with two-thirds believing corporate corruption is endemic.

> EMPLOYEE SURVEYS CONSISTENTLY FIND THAT OVER HALF OF EMPLOYEES CONSIDER THEIR BOSSES TO BE BELOW-AVERAGE LEADERS.

Is it just me, or are these statistics truly alarming? Have people become so conditioned to mediocre leadership that it has become acceptable? Don't people realize that economic recessions, company layoffs, and many other societal issues that negatively affect them are rooted in mediocre leadership? Don't leaders understand the high costs of employee disengagement and turnover they are causing?

Family studies are not much better. Many studies find that the majority of parents don't adequately parent their children. Many children grow up without the essential capabilities they need to become self-sufficient and responsible members of society.

In regard to the impact of leadership on business performance, after adjusting for economic conditions, average company financial results are generating historically low returns on assets and investments. Executive and employee turnover is at an all-time high, with two of every three employees seriously considering leaving their organizations. Over two-thirds of company projects fail to meet expectations. Business bankruptcies continue to increase with typical organizational longevity now being measured in years rather than decades. Employees are less engaged. Morale is down. Job stress is up. It wasn't very long ago that *adrenal fatigue* and *fibromyalgia* weren't in the business vernacular. By many measures, business performance continues to get worse.

Many people in leadership positions today are less qualified to lead than their predecessors from previous generations. Of course there are exceptions, but many contemporary leaders are mediocre at best by historical standards. Some, frankly, are incompetent. They lack experience in dealing with adversity, the ability to motivate people, and countless other important leadership qualities. It seems almost the norm now that parents aren't parenting their children, managers aren't leading their employees, and public servants aren't serving their public.

Perhaps the most obvious impact of poor leadership is in government and public service. As I was writing this book series, there were an unprecedented number of political uprisings around the world because citizens were exasperated by their incompetent and corrupt government officials. The leaders in some governments are so inept that citizens are giving their lives for the hope of new leadership for their countries. Even in democratically elected governments such as the United States, members of Congress are routinely ousted from their positions as they are caught in illicit behavior, conspiracy, and other felonious acts. It seems to be the norm rather than the exception that members of Congress put their own agendas first, their party's agendas second, and the best interests of the citizens of the United States at a distant third priority. They seem to be more concerned about maintaining their public image, power, and control than serving the public—not what most citizens consider good leadership.

Poor leadership often results from people being elected into public office and hired into senior management positions based on positive initial impressions. Many people have the ability to tell a good story and deliver an articulate message, at least initially. By all outward appearances, they seem to be good leadership material. Yet after they are in their role for a short period of time their true leadership competence, or lack thereof, is exposed. What initially appeared to be great leadership ability turns out to be a facade. Unless they are lucky enough to ride the wave of success initiated by their predecessors or they benefit from other fortuitous circumstances, their leadership veneer wears off and their true leadership ability is revealed. Too few people in positions of influence appear to be good leaders on the outside and back it up with true leadership competence from the inside.

Many managers give lip service to the qualities and behaviors of great leadership. Managers claim to focus on long-term results, yet they make decisions as if next year doesn't matter. They say innovation is critical to their organization's success while humiliating people for making mistakes. They state that employees are their top priority but don't budget for employee training or professional development programs. It is easy for managers to say what people want to hear but not so easy to put it into practice and produce the results that are truly possible. For too many managers, the reality is that they are not the caliber of leader they think they are. Neither are they the leaders their people wish they would be.

There are many bureaucrats, bosses, and managers in the world but few leaders and even fewer great leaders. The obvious question is "Why?" From my experience in coaching hundreds of executives, there are many reasons behind the dearth of great leadership—some defensible and some not. Here are my top ten.

1. **Busyness:** People are chronically busy trying to do more, often with less. Expectations of productivity and performance continue to rise but without commensurate improvements in methods, tools, facilities, systems, and processes.

   Compounding the problem is the increasing pace of change. New technologies come out daily. Markets shift by the minute. It is a full-time job just to monitor information feeds, stay current on important events, and follow developing news. People are constantly distracted because distractions have become a societal and business norm.

   Rarely do people find ways to do less. Instead, people continue to find ways to do more. People no longer take a two-minute crosstown train trip or wait in line at the grocery store without checking or sending messages. People are so reactive and tactically focused that they can't focus on strategic activity such as developing their leadership skills.

2. **Fear and Insecurity:** People fear responsibility, particularly those who have low self-esteem. Fear of looking foolish, legal liability, or public dissent prevent many people from leading and taking ownership. If a decision is likely to be unpopular, no matter how right and necessary it might be, people tend not to make it. The first question many people ask isn't "What is right?" but "What will others think?" or "What is the legal risk?" The risk of being embarrassed, saying something politically incorrect, being judged in the court of public opinion, or being sued prevent people from doing or saying what truly needs to be done or said.

   Insecurity also causes managers to become more ego-centric. Insecurity makes managers exercise their authority if for no reason other than to offset their lack of confidence. Managers with low self-esteem are easily offended and frequently feel they are under attack. They are quick to retaliate rather than think logically because they lack the self-confidence to stay calm. They express sarcasm and belittle others to make themselves feel more important. They also tend to be constantly stressed, which causes them to use bad judgment and make bad decisions.

3. **Selfishness:** People are more concerned than ever about themselves and their immediate stakeholders than about the broader good. When given the chance to do something good for their country, public servants instead make decisions based on what's good for their district. Managers make decisions based on what's best for their team rather than the whole organization. Parents, community leaders, employees,

and others in a position of influence do what is best for themselves even when it is at odds with what is best for others and the broader population. Hence minority interests receive more emphasis than those from the majority, and the good of the broader population incrementally declines.

4. **Limited Consequences:** There are few consequences for bad leadership. Politicians make promises they don't keep and face few repercussions for it. Managers don't develop their people, yet when their people underperform, it becomes the employees' fault. Children misbehave at school and are sent to detention, but their parents take no responsibility for their behavior. By simply hiring a divorce attorney, spouses can quickly get out of their marriage vows.

    I want to ask: Why aren't parents put into detention instead of their misbehaving children? Why aren't politicians fined or put in jail for lying? Why aren't managers held accountable for their bad hiring decisions and employee incompetence? Why aren't spouses held accountable in some way for violating their marriage vows? Without consequences, there is little motivation to lead and act responsibly.

5. **Effort:** People want everything fast and easy. They have little patience for long-term initiatives such as leadership development. People expect to learn all they need to know through on-the-job experience or perhaps by reading a few books or attending an occasional seminar. There is little appetite for a year-long or multiyear investment.

    For those who do make the learning investment, many fall short in application. They don't make the vital transition from knowing to doing, and so their knowledge is left unapplied. They can't handle the discomfort of changing their behavior or the inconvenience associated with practicing new skills and habits.

People's lack of effort is fueled by popular positive psychology that says people should always be happy. There is a widespread sentiment that people don't have to focus on what they can't do—all they have to do is focus on what they want and what they can do. The idea is that somehow, what people don't do well miraculously becomes irrelevant and what they want just happens. While happiness is a great quality to have, happiness shouldn't come at the expense of self-improvement.

As a result of people's short-term focus and avoidance of discomfort, they take in the *why* and the *what* of leadership but shy away from the *how*. They fall victim to the huge gap between knowing and doing—the *why* and *what* versus the *how*. The *why* of something is inspiring, intriguing, and often entertaining. Knowing why someone volunteers for a charity, starts their own business, or pursues a particular hobby reveals fascinating insights about them. The *what* of something appeals to people's desire for knowledge and makes for good discussion. Knowing what someone did to earn a promotion, close a sale, or ruin a friendship makes for good conversation and debate. The *how* of something is the point where content gets too detailed for most people. The *how* is where people have to move their knowledge into understanding and application. It is where audiences start to yawn or fall asleep. It is where the real effort is required to become a great leader, and so people tend to avoid it.

6. **Lack of Approach:** Leading is very different from a domain skill such as engineering, selling, or marketing. In these fields, there are straightforward processes to follow. Leadership is different. There is no standard leadership process that a person follows. Leaders never know what step they are on because there aren't any steps. They don't have the diagnostic

framework a doctor has or the planning framework a project manager has.

Despite thousands of leadership programs and models, few provide a simple yet functional approach like those provided for professionals in other domains. Leadership programs that do get into the level of detail required to teach someone how to become a great leader often don't provide the details in a model that is easy to follow. People learn what to do but then struggle to put it into application because they lack an easy-to-use reference model.

7. **Lack of Practicality:** Even fewer leadership programs and models are practical. It is a primary reason for the disconnect in most organizations between their competency models and how managers actually operate. Leadership isn't about knowing concepts, complying with policies, or following procedures. Leadership isn't about using strengths. It's far more demanding than that. Leadership is situational—dependent on an almost unlimited number of variables and circumstances. Simple and theoretical leadership models may be appealing, as they give the illusion of a quick path to great leadership, but true leadership and developing leadership competence isn't that simple.

8. **No Standard:** Unlike becoming a registered engineer, certified public accountant, or licensed hair stylist, there is no formal certification for becoming a leader. There are no standard expectations of performance or objective tests that measure proficiency. Many people claim to be leaders when in reality they are more managers, if not the lucky beneficiaries of fortuitous circumstances. Without a standard of performance to compare to or objective competency assessment to take, people can simply claim to be leaders, even great leaders, and ignore the need to develop any further.

9. **Task Focus:** Effective leadership requires strong interpersonal skills, yet many managers are better equipped to deal with tasks than people. Too many managers focus on projects, proposals, bids, budgets, reports, and deadlines instead of people. Individual contributors are often promoted into management based on their domain expertise, which they continue to rely on despite moving into management.

   Cultures and management systems also neglect people. Even organizations that ostensibly promote people-centric philosophies often implement their people-centric programs as single tasks instead of ongoing processes. When their programs are completed, managers go back to their normal operational duties and largely neglect their people and their people's need for ongoing professional development. Too many managers see their subordinates as a small part of their responsibility, if not just one task of many, and therefore don't truly lead, much less coach.

10. **Management Versus Coaching Focus:** When managers do spend time with their people, they focus on directing and managing them instead of developing them. Studies consistently find that the number one management behavior employees find most valuable is coaching, yet their managers don't coach them or facilitate their development. Managers don't truly get to know their employees' developmental needs and don't help them develop on an individual and sustained basis. Organizations claim that their people are their most valuable assets, yet managers do little to develop their most valuable assets. They don't back up their "most valuable asset" rhetoric with commensurate time, effort, and money.

   Senior leaders are rarely any better. Senior leaders don't get to know their junior managers' needs or help them develop. Worse, senior leaders often foster a climate that makes managers afraid to say they don't know something or admit their need for professional development. The end result is that many managers never receive the coaching or mentoring they need to become the great leaders many of them can be. If it weren't for the perfunctory annual appraisal process in many organizations, many senior leaders and junior managers alike would never have professional development conversations with their employees at all.

These issues are the real challenges to great leadership and the ones that the SCOPE of Leadership book series directly targets. The SCOPE of Leadership framework is designed to overcome these issues. It directly contends with busyness, fear, insecurity, and selfishness. It provides a standard framework and practical approach that makes taking leadership responsibility and putting in the required effort straightforward. It promotes a people-centered approach and, in particular, a coaching approach, which gives employees their much-needed and desired ongoing individual professional development.

FOCUS ON THAT WHICH PRODUCES RESULTS

John Wooden was one of the most successful coaches of any sport in history. He won ten college basketball national championships and nineteen conference championships, oversaw four undefeated seasons, and finished his forty-year career with an 81 percent winning record. Interestingly, UCLA's most successful college basketball coach never told his team to "go win" but rather to simply do their very best. He knew that if his team played their best, they would win. There was a simple but profound principle he followed and one of the most important principles of leadership—you don't get results by focusing on results but rather by focusing on that which produces results.

Managers frequently work at their peak capacity and still don't get everything done. Some work so hard they make themselves physically ill. Others become chronically stressed out trying to meet their deadlines, complete all their work, and reach their performance targets. Many develop performance anxiety because they focus predominately on the goals rather than on what achieves the goals. Their stress becomes so severe that they feel overwhelmed, their performance declines, and they further impede their ability to reach the very goals they so desperately seek.

You can focus on either results or that which produces results. The highest-performing leaders focus on that which produces results. They encourage, coach, and enable the attributes in their people that in turn produce the desired results. Rather than telling their people to produce an outcome like win a basketball game, great leaders focus on helping people develop the attitudes and behaviors required to win the game.

The behaviors that lead to results deserve your focus, not the results themselves. Because I frequently work with sales teams, I often encounter unknowing sales managers who create incentive awards for their salespeople to reach their sales targets, which are based on results, not behaviors. Instead of focusing their salespeople on improving their selling behaviors, they simply focus their people on the results. When the sales contest is over, most of their salespeople have little improved skill or knowledge to show for the effort and stress they invested. Had the managers created incentives for desired behaviors in addition to results, salespeople would have both achieved the results the sales managers were looking for as well as refined and improved the desirable behaviors.

> THE BEHAVIORS THAT LEAD TO RESULTS DESERVE YOUR FOCUS, NOT THE RESULTS THEMSELVES.

When you focus on that which produces results, you not only put the focus on the right activity, but you also do it with less stress. In contrast, when you constantly think about your goal, like winning a contest, you become anxious, which is not helpful to achieving your goal. Instead of focusing on building the behaviors needed to win the contest, you worry about winning the contest. Rather than taking it one step or day at a time, you concentrate on the end result. Rather than concentrate on what you are doing, you think about what is left to be done.

By focusing on that which produces results, you live in the present moment. You focus on being the best you can be now. You put your full attention and energy on the task at hand. You work and perform without the distraction and stress that come with thinking about what you have left to do to reach your desired result.

The key to working in the present is giving your immediate work your best effort and knowing that you are giving your current work your best. When you are applying all the knowledge, skill, and effort you reasonably can, you know the results will take care of themselves. You know there is nothing more you can give, so you don't worry about anything else—including the results.

The same principle applies when leading people. When everyone on a team gives their best, you don't have to worry about the team's results. The team produces the best results possible. That is the reason great leaders focus on their people and their people's behaviors rather than simply telling them to go produce a result. Telling someone to produce a result is ineffective. It puts focus on the anxiety of winning rather than on result-producing behaviors. It does nothing to help people actually develop. It does nothing to improve the likelihood that they will actually succeed.

Results are achieved through people's behaviors; therefore, great leaders focus on people. Coaching, encouraging, and enabling the right behaviors and attitudes in people are how great leaders achieve goals and produce results. Not inconsequentially, the best results also come with the least amount of stress. Unknown to many managers who are chronically stressed is that there is a much more effective and less stressful way to lead.

If you aspire to achieve anything great, including becoming a great leader, focus on the enablers to your goal, not the goal itself. That is the reason great leadership isn't just about casting a vision or setting an expectation. It isn't merely holding people accountable to some number or goal. Great leaders like John Wooden coach, encourage, and enable their people. They employ a coaching approach to leadership and focus on desired behaviors, which in turn produce desired results.

WHO NEEDS LEADERSHIP?

With the dearth of great leadership in the world, you might wonder if organizations wouldn't be better off without leadership. However, while ineffective leadership is bad, so is no leadership. Most people don't naturally exercise good judgment, sustain a disciplined work ethic, maintain self-control, continuously improve, and work with their teammates for the good of the whole team.

Without leadership, most people take the path of least resistance. They stay in their comfort zone and underleverage their capabilities. They underperform and cause the team to underperform. Organizations, teams, and families without leadership are like ships without rudders. If they do achieve acceptable levels of performance, it is more often through lucky circumstances or only after wasting excessive resources and time to get there.

The absence of leadership causes many dysfunctions. People become selfish and look out for their own interests instead of what's best for the team. Cooperation is replaced with competition, bickering, and conflict. Whining replaces problem solving. Blaming replaces ownership. Fear and inaction replace engagement. Stress, absenteeism, low morale, high turnover, and inconsistency become the norm. People might work reasonably well on their own without leadership, but they rarely work the best they can as a team.

The importance of leadership is found in every facet of society. Parenting is one of the best examples: studies find that children raised in single-parent households, where children receive significantly less parenting, are twice as likely to end up incarcerated as those who grow up in two-parent households. Over half of the inmates in state correctional facilities grew up without the leadership provided by a two-parent household.

Professional sports teams that consistently outperform their competition consistently have a strong team leader or a great coach. Organizations that consistently achieve their goals consistently have strong leaders. Federal, state, and local governments that maintain balanced budgets and vibrant economies are led by competent leaders. It is no coincidence that the most inept and corrupt country leaders in the world lead countries with the highest levels of poverty, highest crime rates, and shortest life expectancy.

A lack of great leadership results in poor performance, whether at home, on the field, in the workplace, or in the community. We can't be our best, safest, or most prosperous without leadership.

IN DEFENSE OF BAD LEADERSHIP

In people's defense, there are many bad role models. History as well as contemporary society is full of shoddy leaders in prominent positions. The infamous in particular make for interesting news, giving them undeservedly high exposure. Their failures and misdoings are widely publicized. Corrupt politicians regularly make the news for violating ethical standards. Promiscuous celebrities get arrested for possession of illegal drugs and their uncontrollable violence in domestic disputes. Shameless professional athletes get caught in infidelity. Greedy corporate executives get caught violating stock-trading regulations. The public's attention is usually on what people shouldn't be doing instead of on what they should be doing. It is with much less frequency that a cover story reports the good deeds that someone does or the great leadership they provide.

Bad examples are publicized not just in the news but also in the workplace. Too often undeserving managers are held up as good examples and promoted into more senior positions. Many were simply at the right place at the right time, were able to tell a good story to the right person, or took credit for someone else's efforts.

At home too many children learn bad behaviors as they watch their parents take pleasure in their addictions, lash out at each other in their arguments, and distort the truth when it is in their best interest to do so. Many people have been conditioned for their entire life, at work and at home, to expect, accept, and imitate the habits of poor leadership.

In contrast to the infamous, most great leaders receive very little publicity. They perform their work behind the scenes with little fanfare. The results of their work show up in others' work. Those they influence are the ones in the spotlight. You see great achievements every day, but you rarely hear about the great parents, spouses, bosses, mentors, or coaches who were leading them in the background.

There is nothing wrong with getting publicity. It is an important part of receiving well-deserved recognition, creating brand awareness, acquiring new customers, and recruiting top performers. However, great leaders don't lead because they want to be in the spotlight. They lead, encourage, coach, and enable to create results, not publicity. Any publicity they receive is secondary to the core purpose of what they do.

Great leadership goes against many natural human tendencies. Great leadership requires that you put others first, often sacrificing your own interests. Great leadership requires that you work through others even when it would be faster and easier for you to do the work yourself. Great leadership is about putting people and values first when you'd rather put projects or short-term results first. It is about deferring gratification, investing in the long term, and making decisions that can be unpopular and inconvenient.

Many of the principles of great leadership are counterintuitive. When you want someone to do something, you don't tell them what to do; you ask questions. When you want to impress someone, you listen instead of talk. Instinct might suggest that you prevent someone from making a mistake or experiencing adverse circumstances, but adversity is exactly what people need in order to learn. Great leaders encourage reasonable risks and tolerate mistakes. You may have a well-developed strength, but in certain situations it is your Achilles' heel. Your engrained habits tell you to do one thing when the exact opposite is a better choice when leading others.

With poor role models and a natural tendency to do the opposite of what is often the better approach, it is easy to understand why there is so much bad leadership.

MYTHS OF LEADERSHIP

Given that great leadership goes against the grain of many human tendencies and contemporary social norms, there are many misunderstandings about leadership. Here are the top ten myths about leadership that I most often encounter.

- **Myth #1: Great leaders are the celebrated people and are widely known.** All types of leaders receive publicity, but the media is not the validating mechanism for great leadership. Many highly publicized CEOs, government officials, coaches, athletes, musicians, TV show hosts, and political activists have earned their publicity more through self-promotion and infamy than through great leadership. In contrast, great leaders don't merely do their best work on a stage or in front of a camera. They work best with and through their children, employees, constituents, and athletes. When great leaders receive publicity, it is usually as part of a great team performance, not as a single individual. Being a celebrity doesn't equal being a great leader.

  THE MEDIA IS NOT THE VALIDATING MECHANISM FOR GREAT LEADERSHIP.

- **Myth #2: Leaders are the senior executives.** Executive positions and titles confer power of position, but titles don't correlate to great leadership. There are as many lower-level managers and employees who are great leaders as there are senior executives who are terrible leaders. Many senior managers discourage their employees and frustrate their customers. Senior managers are fired daily for their poor leadership. Studies find that the higher the position that people attain and the more power they gain, the more likely they are to rely on power rather than skill to influence others, and the more likely they are to ignore leadership best practices and become elitist. Lofty titles and authority have a way of eroding people's compassion, humility, availability, and ultimately their effectiveness. Leadership is a blend of attitudes and aptitudes that are independent of power and position. Leadership is not defined by people's roles but by what they do in those roles.

- **Myth #3: Leadership is not as important as having talented individuals on the team.** If only this were true. In theory it sounds great, but in reality it takes leadership to get teams to perform to their peak potential. The leadership might not come from the top of the organization, but at some level there are people who coach, enable, and encourage others. A high-performing team without a leader is a rare exception. This is not to say that high performance is solely due to leadership. Clearly it takes hardworking, competent people for a team to succeed, but without leadership, teams don't reach their highest performance. As with sports teams, community and workplace teams that are led by great leaders outperform those that aren't.

- **Myth #4: Leaders are born, not made.** Leaders are made, not born. They are made through experience, adversity, education, and determination. Leadership is available to anyone willing to make the sacrifices that leadership requires. It is a learned behavior, not a genetic byproduct. Unlike popularized stereotypes, the greatest leaders don't have the highest IQs, limitless natural talent, thick dark hair, and above-average height. There are many smart people who woefully underperform. Leadership is not limited to the fortunate few who come from a royal bloodline or are descendants of highly successful people. In fact the opposite happens—many children of great leaders become entitled, arrogant, lacking in experience, and miserable failures. Anyone can be a great leader as much as anyone can be a great failure.

- **Myth #5: Leadership is not as important as having great strategies, sound business processes, and robust systems.** In the mid-twentieth century, W. Edwards Deming, considered the father of quality control and process improvement, attributed the majority of performance problems to poor systems, strategies, and processes. His philosophy has been amplified ever since through quality and process-improvement programs. What people don't realize is that processes, systems, and strategies are dependent on the people who conceive and implement them. You can't have great strategies, processes, and systems without people and great leadership.

- **Myth #6: Leaders aren't managers.** While leading and managing are two very different competencies, great leaders are also great managers. There are few leaders who don't also perform the role of manager. Leaders don't always lead. There are times they follow and times they simply need to manage what is already in place rather than create something new or lead people in a different direction. Great leaders know when they shouldn't make changes as clearly as they know when they should. Because the best leadership approach for a given situation varies with the situation, great leaders employ multiple leadership approaches, including a management approach when it is required.

- **Myth #7: Leadership is an art and can't be made into a science.** Leadership is both art and science. The problem with making science out of leadership is that it is inherently intangible and complex. It is situational. However, just because people don't take the time to understand the science behind human behavior doesn't mean science doesn't exist and can't be applied. Like building a house, the most effective way to build leadership competence follows a structured approach that includes creating a plan, establishing a strong foundation, building a quality infrastructure, and finishing it off with an attractive facade. This still leaves flexibility for the art—different architectures and furnishings, just like great leadership allows for people's individual styles and uniqueness. Adding to this support for leadership as a science are many recent advances in behavioral science. Improvements in understanding how the human brain works are increasingly making leadership more tangible and scientific.

- **Myth #8: Leadership can be boiled down to a few simple principles.** Leadership is multidimensional and situational. It is wide-ranging and dynamic. It can't be adequately defined or learned through a few simple principles. It can be taught, understood, and learned, but not by merely following a few core values or general philosophies. Still, people try to make it simple. They treat leadership like the latest fad diet or fitness device, as if learning leadership were as simple as spending five minutes a day using a contraption to build ripped abdominal muscles. It is no wonder that inexperienced managers who try to follow simple suggestions become confused, if not cynical, about leadership. Leadership is well within the realm of comprehension, but like most any profession, it can't be effectively performed by only following a few precepts.

- **Myth #9: The goal of leadership is to make money.** Goals are different for different people. Goals can be financial, professional, relational, social, spiritual, or physical. Leadership is *success-neutral*. Leadership is about achieving results, not necessarily financial results. It takes great leadership to promote a new product, raise responsible children, develop a vibrant community, and maintain a faithful congregation. It takes great leadership to complete a project on time, build products to high-quality specifications, or lead loved ones through a family crisis. Great leaders are focused on achieving a desired outcome, not necessarily with making more money.

- **Myth #10: Leadership is the end goal.** Leadership is the means to a goal, not a goal in itself. Leadership is how you achieve results. Leadership is working in, through, and with people to achieve an outcome that would be impossible on your own and is greater than what others could achieve on their own. If you're not moving people toward a meaningful goal, you are not leading. Leading people without a focus on producing results is merely activity. It is busyness. It is arrogance. The purpose of leadership isn't to gain power so you can exercise your ego. Leadership isn't about earning the right to control people. It isn't about impressive titles, corner offices, or country club memberships. If you aspire to be a leader for the purpose of status, fame, or fortune, you will be a disappointment to yourself and your team. Great leadership is about producing results. Any stature or fame achieved from great leadership is the byproduct of great leadership, not its goal. Leadership is the means to achieving a desired outcome.

> LEADERSHIP IS THE MEANS TO A GOAL, NOT A GOAL IN ITSELF.

THE MEASURE OF LEADERSHIP

Few areas have more impact on an organization's performance than leadership, yet leadership on its own is intangible. Its effect can't be denied, but it is not directly measurable. The real impact of great leadership comes through the results of those whom leaders influence, not the leader's own individual contribution.

Evaluating leadership effectiveness involves looking at the results of the leader's sphere of influence. Leadership effectiveness is the difference between how a team would perform on its own and how it performs under its leader's influence. It is leaders' impact on their teams' efficiency, production, quality, attitude, skill development, and results.

Leadership effectiveness is the measure of what happens as a result of leaders' influence. It is the difference in the condition before and after of the organization, department, neighborhood, city, county, state, country, or family they lead. It is the measure of their impact on areas such as those listed in Table 1.1.

TABLE 1.1: MEASURES OF LEADERSHIP EFFECTIVENESS

• Profit	• Operational efficiency
• Sales	• Asset utilization
• Customer satisfaction	• Return on investment
• Partner satisfaction	• Cost containment
• Employee morale	• Employee sense of responsibility
• Teamwork	• Employee sense of urgency
• Environmental stewardship	• Employee pride and self-esteem
• Community improvement	• Decision-making quality
• Employee turnover	• Employee engagement
• Internal promotions	• Employee skill development
• Employee productivity	• Product quality

- Competitive differentiation
- Strategy formulation
- Progress toward vision
- Communication flow
- Talent utilization
- Adoption of organizational values

Great leaders positively impact these performance areas. The assessment of a leader's effectiveness should therefore be based on how much his or her influence impacts these results. Although leaders don't control every variable and circumstance that impacts their organization, they influence how their people react to the variables and circumstances. The actions leaders take, as well as the actions they choose not to take, impact their organization's performance. That is the reason it is customary for leaders to receive the blame as well as the credit for what happened in their organization, regardless of the cause.

Measuring the quality of leadership is made even more difficult by money and contracts. Professional coaches and corporate managers have a crutch. Athletes and employees follow their coaches and managers if for no other reason than because they are contractually obligated to do so or because they won't get paid if they don't. Contrast these paid employees to volunteers who follow leaders of nonprofit charities. Volunteers follow by choice. A true test of great leadership lies in how well the leader's inherent ability to influence causes people to take action and produce results by choice. It lies in how well people make the choice to adopt an organizational initiative, develop their skills, or give their best effort without the influence of bonuses, awards, contracts, or continued employment. Consider the extent to which others would follow you and take direction from you if they weren't paid to do so or if you didn't have any authority over them. This reveals the extent of your true leadership effectiveness.

Another measure of leadership effectiveness is how well a leader's followers perform after the leader is gone. You have reached the highest level of leadership when you have embedded sustainable high-performance behaviors into your people and the fabric of your organization. You are truly a great leader when you have transferred your knowledge, competence, and passion to others to the extent that they no longer need you. It may not feel very rewarding when you are no longer in the critical path of an organization's daily activity, but if your employees operate at the highest level without you because you enabled, empowered, and coached them to do so, that is the ultimate reward deserving of the highest evaluation.

When people refer to leadership qualities, they use phrases like *instilling passion*, *shaping the culture*, and *fostering teamwork*. These qualities, like most other leadership qualities, are intangibles. Intangibles such as culture, values, passion, teamwork, and attitudes produce great performance. A successful company's competitive advantage is rooted in intangibles like passionate people, a collaborative spirit, and an ability to innovate continuously. Any cynic who believes value has to be tangible for it to be real needs to look no further than examples like these. Like the wind, you might not be able to see a leader's contributions directly, but the effects are undeniable.

While great leadership isn't always obvious, poor leadership is easy to see. As opposed to well-led organizations where activities run smoothly without drawing much attention to them, poorly led organizations draw a lot of attention. Poor leadership causes poor communication, frustration, bickering, internal competition, bureaucracy, politics, and gossip. In poorly led organizations, employees are noticeably disengaged and apathetic. Their results are inconsistent. Employees are unsure of their roles, responsibilities, and level of authority. They have to ask regularly for guidance or permission to perform their work. Employees work primarily in react mode because they have to contend constantly with quality and operational issues. Employee passion and enthusiasm are largely absent. Confidence is displaced by fear. Teamwork is exchanged for conflict.

THE NEED TO LEAD AS A COACH

The effectiveness of leadership shows up in the quality of relationships between managers and employees. Some relationships are collaborative, while others are merely cooperative and some are outright competitive. Some are vibrant, while others are antagonistic. There are managers and employees who have great respect for each other and work closely together like committed partners, but others hardly see each other—or wish they never did.

Employee–manager relationships depend on many factors related to the manager's leadership effectiveness, the employee's performance, and organizational influences. An organization's culture, HR policies, and HR systems have an impact. The manager's leadership style, span of responsibility, and leadership competence have an impact. The employee's level of performance, skill level, role, and attitude have an impact. More than any other factor, however, managers and their leadership approach determine the nature of the employee–manager relationship.

Some managers operate as *supercontributors* who are individual contributors, albeit with a higher level of responsibility. They often have a peer-level relationship with their employees. Other managers act like stereotypical military commanders who tell their people where to go, what to do, and how to do it. They are *taskmasters* who have an authoritarian relationship with their employees. Some managers act as charismatic politicians who make endearing promises and strive for popularity by telling people what they want to hear. They are *chameleons* who have a superficial relationship with their employees. Some managers are disengaged and not materially involved in managing or leading at all. They are *phantom* managers having virtually no relationship with their employees.

The basis of the SCOPE of Leadership is that the most effective relationship and approach a manager can employ is akin to one of a coach working with an athlete. It is a coaching style of management that utilizes coaching best practices. A coaching style inspires and enables people to be their best. It doesn't rely on commands, coercion, or intimidation. Leaders as coaches encourage their employees to be their best, enable them to be their best, and hold them accountable for being their best. They help their employees develop and improve their skills. They establish a nurturing and motivating relationship with their employees as opposed to an adversarial or superficial one.

> A COACHING STYLE INSPIRES AND ENABLES PEOPLE TO BE THEIR BEST.

Virtually every professional athlete, professional musician, professional speaker, and professional politician has a professional coach. It is almost unimaginable that any top performer or sports team can reach the highest level of performance without a coach. Does it not therefore also make sense that working professionals and organizations could benefit from having a coach? Does it not make sense for managers to be a coach to their employees?

If you are unconvinced, consider these top ten reasons why managers should lead as coaches and develop a coaching approach to leadership:

1. **Employees are an organization's most important asset.** Managers spend weeks if not months recruiting, interviewing, and hiring top talent to put on their team. Employees are an organization's most important asset and worth the investment.

2. **Coaching improves employee and organizational performance.** Organizations need higher-skilled employees. Studies find that over three-fourths of organizations have a skills shortfall that prevents them from reaching their goals. Helping to improve people's skills has to be a manager's top priority. Studies also find that employees who receive coaching perform up to 200 percent better than employees

who don't. Regardless of how capable people are, they benefit from a leader's ongoing encouragement, insight, facilitation, enablement, and accountability.

3. **Employees want the help.** Surveys regularly find the top attribute most desired by employees in their manager is an ability to coach. Employees want individualized help in improving their skills. Employees want to learn what their managers know. Employees want to improve their performance.

4. **Annual reviews are not a substitute for coaching.** Annual performance reviews are pathetically insufficient in helping employees improve their performance. Employees and managers need to spend time together regularly on the employee's professional development.

5. **Measurements are not a substitute for coaching.** People need ongoing attention, facilitation, and redirection in how they achieve their results. The correction and recognition that come after results have been recorded are too late to impact the results positively.

6. **Operations conversations are not coaching conversations.** Manager conversations with employees about sales forecasts, budgets, project statuses, and other operational issues don't get to the root issues that prevent people from performing their best.

7. **Basic skills are not practiced without recurring reinforcement.** Practicing and honing fundamental skills differentiate good performers from top performers. Yet employees don't regularly practice and work on their skills without the exhortation and attention that comes with coaching.

8. **Top performers value the development.** A primary reason that top performers join an organization and subsequently stay with an organization is the potential for professional growth. Top performers place great value on learning and development. "Best places to work" surveys consistently praise the winning organizations' talent-development programs.

9. **Managers don't scale.** A manager is one person and can do only so much. If managers expect to get more done, they must work through people. The best contribution they can make isn't their direct contribution but their enabling of others who make the direct contributions.

    If you are the type of manager who believes the more important contribution you provide is helping to do your team's work rather than coaching the team to do it themselves, realize this—you don't scale. Fortunately your team does, and as they develop their skills, their performance will improve and the team will grow. Your capacity is extremely limited compared to the capacity of your team. Your best investment is in coaching your team to be as good as or better than yourself. One top-performing manager is not a substitute for a team of equally top-performing employees.

10. **Your competitors, market, and company aren't static.** The world constantly changes. People must continually learn, develop, and adapt to stay current. When your market changes and your competitors adapt, but you don't, you fall behind. When you don't learn new skills and don't continually improve, you fall behind.

Bonus:

Coaching leaves a legacy. When successful people are asked about the aspects of their career that most enabled their success, they consistently mention a mentor, athletic coach, or boss who took the time to work with them individually on their development.

If you care about your reputation and the legacy you will leave as a leader, know that it will be based on the extent to which you developed and mentored others more than any other quality you possess or result you produce.

COMPLACENCY

A *new normal* developed in the late twentieth century and early twenty-first century. The nature of societies, economies, industries, and jobs changed forever. How people communicate, interact, work, and play changed to an extreme not seen since the industrial revolution of the nineteenth century.

There were many contributing factors that caused the new normal. Demographic changes, overextended markets, economic recessions, a significant increase in the cost of fuel, a dramatic decrease in the cost of communications, public sentiment toward environmental stewardship, and government policies all played a part. However, the impact of those paled in comparison to the most significant contributor—advances in science, technology, and engineering that produced the Internet.

The Internet and its offspring of life-changing applications created massive shifts in how the world works. The Internet's disruptive effects changed every aspect of life. Information became ubiquitous. Distance became meaningless in many contexts. Productivity jumped dramatically. Scale became possible without size. The very nature of what people did that constituted value changed. Customers, suppliers, and employees became empowered. People had more options, new choices, and unbounded opportunity.

Distribution channels changed from physical to electronic. Geographic borders became less important. Access to information became untethered and ubiquitous. Industries like health care, advertising, publishing, transportation, and entertainment were completely transformed. Entire industries of brokers, wholesalers, and agents were disintermediated. New markets were created and old ones perished. Many jobs went away forever while new ones were born.

Perhaps most importantly, the new normal removed the chains from change. Physical limitations that had constrained the pace and nature of change were lifted. As digital means eliminated physical limitations, change became unbridled. The respites from change that existed before were replaced with constant change. Now no one escapes the need to change, grow, and develop if they expect to remain relevant and keep up. In the new normal, no one gets by with complacency.

Complacency for any extended period of time is commensurate with obsolescence. No longer can people rest on past successes, skills, or knowledge. People can't stay in the confines of their comfort zones. People can't be repetitive creatures of habit and machines of mindless execution and expect to remain up to date. This applies to people in every domain or role, including management and leadership.

> COMPLACENCY FOR ANY EXTENDED PERIOD OF TIME IS COMMENSURATE WITH OBSOLESCENCE.

Managers who have not kept up and embraced the new normal have been ejected by companies at a swift pace. In the transition to the new normal, millions of people, including many managers, lost their jobs and found limited prospects for new ones. They looked for management jobs as they had before but found that those jobs were gone. The new normal didn't pay managers to act merely as conduits of information or facilitators of meetings. The new normal didn't need managers merely to organize, manage, administer, allocate, disseminate, report, count, track, transact, or oversee. These roles were largely displaced by automation and electronic transactions.

Unless you are financially secure and permanently retired, don't allow yourself to become complacent. To remain relevant and fulfill the need to lead, continue to learn. Continue to grow and adapt. Enjoy and leverage rather than resist the incredible lifestyle improvements and opportunities that are part of the new normal.

Complacency is a dead end. It ruins not only leadership careers but also marriages and lives. Avoid losing your domain fluency and relevance. Accept that you must continuously learn and grow. Don't settle for tired old routines of outdated management practices. Don't be satisfied with what you currently know and do. It leads only to obsolescence. To become and remain a great leader, embrace change.

CREATING THE FUTURE

While the effects of poor leadership are obvious when you know what to look for, many people don't see them. Because of the dearth of great leaders, people have come to expect poor leadership and have lowered their standards. Rather than being surprised when they encounter a poor leader, people are surprised when they encounter a great leader. It is a shameful validation of our contemporary society's mediocre standards of leadership.

Yet the importance of great leadership can't be overstated. Our collective future is as bright as our leadership pipeline is full of great leaders. The success of our organizations, families, and communities is dependent upon how well people step up to the challenge of becoming great leaders. We need responsible, competent, and influential people at all organizational, societal, and governmental levels if we expect to remain vibrant, competitive, and successful.

The greatest threat to our businesses, families, and communities is from the inside. There will always be aggressive competitors, unfortunate accidents, disruptive weather patterns, and selfish scoundrels trying to take advantage of us. We can't control these circumstances, so our success depends on how well we contend with and overcome them. Our future success isn't dependent on eliminating external issues as much as it is on knowing how to contend with them, which in turn depends on great leadership.

Left unaddressed, our leadership crisis will continue to erode our competitiveness and our quality of life. Unresolved, poor leadership will ultimately wear away our basic freedoms as we succumb to being followers instead of leaders. This is the reason there isn't much that is more important than ensuring our families, schools, businesses, churches, organizations, communities, and countries are led by effective leaders. We need great leadership now and a pipeline of great leaders for the future.

If this isn't obvious to you, consider the negative impact caused by corrupt politicians and selfish executives. During the scandal-plagued first decade of the twenty-first century, millions of people lost their jobs and retirement savings due to corrupt leaders. Leaders of companies such as WorldCom, Enron, and Bernard L. Madoff Investment Securities caused massive financial losses for individuals. People lost their jobs, retirement accounts, and homes.

Think, too, about the impact of incompetent parents who don't lead and properly parent their children. Our jails are full of irresponsible people whose parents never taught them how to behave, treat people, and respect property. Reckless behavior and bad leadership take a huge toll on society.

The good news is that leadership is a learned behavior. It is within anyone's grasp. It takes effort to develop but is no more difficult than learning most any trade or profession. If you simply accept the calling and responsibility to lead, you can become a great leader. Over time you can learn to lead like a great leader, and as you do, you will develop other leaders—who in turn will develop others. As with a powerful viral marketing message, great leadership will spread like an epidemic. A wave of great leaders will emerge, all but wiping out our leadership crisis.

THE BEST INVESTMENT YOU CAN MAKE

Everyone experiences the effects of leadership, both good and bad. Employees, customers, suppliers, partners, and investors are all impacted by the decisions and actions of leaders. The roads you drive on, the freedoms you have, the products you use, and the foods you eat are just a few of the daily experiences you either enjoy or become frustrated with because of a leader's influence. Whether you enjoy your work or see it as a chore largely depends on the leadership of the organization you work for. When something works well—or doesn't—there is a leader's influence at the root of it.

An unfortunate casualty of poor leadership is that it turns people away from becoming leaders themselves. Studies find that three out of four employees have no interest in attaining their boss's position. Because so many managers do a poor job of setting the right example of what a leader should do, people don't want to become leaders. Employees don't want to become like their stressed-out and overworked boss; they don't want to have to do the extra work, put in the extra hours, take on the extra responsibility, and become as disingenuous or cynical as their boss might be. Employees don't realize that great leadership isn't doing people's work for them but rather is caring for, coaching, encouraging, and enabling people. If people knew what great leadership truly was, they would see it as the truly great job it is and be more interested in pursuing it.

As I was writing this book, there was a movement of protesters occupying parks in major cities across the United States and demonstrating over a variety of issues related to what they felt were corporate injustices. What was most interesting about this was that rather than lead in a constructive way, these protesters chose to protest in an unconstructive way. It revealed a widespread sentiment that many people have about leadership. Many people don't like it and don't want it. Because of people's bad experiences with poor leadership, they equate leadership with selfishness and excess.

Know that selfishness and excess are not qualities of great leaders. Don't let the bad qualities of people in positions of influence dissuade you from becoming a leader. Use bad leadership to motivate rather than demotivate you. Make a decision to help improve the future. Society and organizations desperately need great leadership. Demand is at an all-time high while supply is at an all-time low. The opportunity is huge. With a commitment to develop yourself and a little effort, you can capitalize on the opportunity. You can become a great leader and influence society in a positive and constructive way.

The best investment you can make is in your leadership development. You benefit from it as well as everyone else whom you influence. It accrues interest to you for the rest of your life and to others long after you are gone. Improving leadership has one of the highest paybacks of any investment you can make.

Leadership is a competence; it is a capability. Like any capability, it improves you. It increases your relevance and makes you more valuable. It increases your net worth, gives you confidence and security, and enriches your life personally and professionally. It is a broadly applicable capability that enhances everything you do. If you haven't thought about the benefits of investing in leadership development, consider it now.

Don't let yourself down by using an excuse like "I don't have the time," which people regularly give for not improving themselves. The truth for most people is that they will never have the time to do anything really valuable if they don't get off their treadmill of *busyness as usual*. The very leadership competence that people lack causes them not to have the time to develop their leadership competence. Managers' undeveloped leadership competence causes them to be chronically busy, chronically stressed out, and overwhelmed.

> THE VERY LEADERSHIP COMPETENCE THAT PEOPLE LACK CAUSES THEM NOT TO HAVE THE TIME TO DEVELOP THEIR LEADERSHIP COMPETENCE.

I hope you will make the time to invest in your leadership development. I hope you will leverage the SCOPE of Leadership framework as well as other leadership books, programs, and resources. When you do, you will find that your improved ability to lead and influence people will free up time and make your life much easier and more enjoyable. You will realize the benefits of higher levels of employee engagement, teamwork, and execution. You will enjoy higher levels of performance with less effort.

Choosing to make the investment in developing leadership competence is one of those life-impacting decisions. It is a strategic decision that is as important as any major life decision can be. Yet it only requires a little time—time that you invest in yourself. Don't worry—the treadmill of busyness will survive without your full-time participation in it.

Don't cheat yourself out of the opportunity to learn, develop, and make a higher-level contribution to your organization. Don't exchange an exciting career opportunity for what may instead become mindless routines of execution. Don't make yourself less valuable by spending all your time working to keep up with the tyranny of the urgent. Don't exchange your intellect, creativity, passion, energy, and future opportunity for undemanding busyness.

Make the strategic decision to invest in yourself and become a great leader. It will benefit not only you but also your family, your employer, and our society.

PRINCIPLES IN REVIEW

Here are key principles from this chapter to keep in mind.

- **Results:** You don't get results by focusing on results but rather by focusing on that which produces results.
- **People:** The roots of all achievement lie in people.
- **Leadership Effectiveness:** Your leadership effectiveness is based on the extent to which your influence improves the performance of other people and produces improved results.

- **Complacency:** Embrace change and continuous improvement. Complacency for any extended period of time is commensurate with obsolescence.
- **Leadership Development:** Invest in yourself and in developing the competencies of great leadership. It is one of the most strategic and important investments you can make.

CHAPTER TWO

CHOOSING TO LEAD

Failing organizations are usually overmanaged and under-led.
—Warren G. Bennis

It was late 2001, about eighteen months after the dot-com bubble burst in early 2000, and the information technology industry was recovering from its economic meltdown. I boarded my flight at Boston's Logan Airport to fly back to Dallas. I was reflecting on the day's activities. As far as interviews go, it seemed the day had been a success. I met with the company president, the executive vice president of human resources, and a division executive. They all treated me with a great deal of respect and were as eager to learn about me as I was to learn about them.

I was interviewing for a division general manager position in the information technology industry. The company had an existing product division and service division they planned to integrate with an anticipated acquisition. The acquisition was in the late stages of due diligence, after which they would enter into a definitive agreement. The new general manager position I was interviewing for would be responsible for integrating the three organizations and operating them as a single division.

The industry was very familiar to me. I had worked in it during my fifteen-year career at IBM and for the last couple of years in the dot-com era at Scient. This new position would leverage my industry knowledge, consulting experience, and industry relationships. It would be an opportunity to build and lead an organization with a great deal of potential. As my plane took off and I reclined in my seat, I felt as if this job was a good fit for me.

I received the job offer the next day, and after working out the remaining details, I accepted it. My employment was scheduled to start within the month.

Less than two weeks later, still prior to coming onboard, I received a call from the company president. The due diligence had uncovered significant issues that were going to stop the acquisition. The company to be acquired had overstated its sales backlog by over 50 percent. It turned out the company to be acquired was about to miss its forecast, causing them to lose a substantial amount of money in the coming quarter.

As the surprise of this announcement set in and my questions started pouring out, the president interrupted me, saying, "But I've got another position to offer you." He went on to describe his other business unit, which had been struggling and was in need of a turnaround. It was the company's financial services division. He asked me if I had any experience in financial services, to which I truthfully replied, "I write checks and go to the bank from time to time." He appreciated my honesty, and we both laughed. After we talked about the new position, he thought I was the right person for the job despite my lack of industry knowledge. It would leverage my skills in turning around underperforming organizations, and having already committed to joining the company, I decided to accept it.

In my new job, I didn't have any industry experience, industry relationships, or product knowledge to rely on. I didn't know any of the acronyms or phraseology embedded in every sentence spoken in this industry. I didn't know any of the key customers, analysts, or competitors, how the products were used, or even how to hold a basic conversation about them with a customer, at least not initially. I had only my management skills and leadership ability to rely on.

Fast-forward eighteen months and the division looked significantly different from when I first took responsibility for it. I replaced many people, including my executive vice president of sales and most of the sales team. I built a new services division to complement our product division. I reengineered business processes, gave people new responsibilities, and instituted cross-departmental activities to facilitate teamwork. I focused on developing people's skills. I coached the entire division on how to articulate a value proposition based on the value of our integrated solutions instead of the features of our products. We added new responsibilities to our customer service team, including providing fee-based services. In short, we made significant enhancements to our offerings, our sales approach, and how we serviced our customers. As a result, we closed out our first full year together with a doubling of our revenue and recorded a 7 percent net margin as opposed to an operating loss the division had recorded the year before. By almost every measure the business was a great success.

I worked there another two years before leaving to start my consulting company, Alpine Link. In those two years, we continued to grow the business and deliver a good profit to the company. The turnaround was sustained, and the business was an ongoing success.

> LEADERSHIP COMPETENCE TRUMPS INDUSTRY EXPERIENCE, PRODUCT KNOWLEDGE, AND DOMAIN SKILLS.

The lesson I learned from this experience was that leadership competence trumps industry experience, product knowledge, and domain skills. Leadership is more important than any other skill a manager can have. Had I continued to rely on my industry knowledge and existing relationships as I had done for most of my career, I might never have realized the true power of leading and coaching. The ability to motivate, coach, enable, and assimilate people into a team is the most powerful capability you can have.

LEADERS VERSUS MANAGERS

When I first met Bob, he had just assumed division management responsibility for a $70 million division within a $450 million construction company. Business had been good for his firm for the last fourteen years. They had enjoyed steady growth in both their commercial and residential construction markets, but almost without warning, the construction market stalled about a year prior to Bob's appointment. His firm's core business went from predictable, steady growth to an unexpected and sharp decline. In just one year, their business revenues dropped by 21 percent and their backlog fell from twenty-eight months of work to less than six months. Their forecast for the next two years called for a continued market contraction of 10 to 25 percent per year.

These were tough times by any standard for Bob and his firm. Market conditions like these test even the best companies and leaders. He would have to make many tough decisions and provide real leadership to navigate the economic uncertainties that were ahead.

Two years later, I concluded my executive coaching engagement with Bob. To mark the occasion, we went out for a steak dinner together and recalled some of the difficult moments Bob had lived through. So much had transpired, it seemed like much more than two years had passed.

In those two years, Bob laid off almost a third of his staff. He renegotiated contracts with suppliers and partners. He sold off properties and shut down non-core-business assets. He acquired two companies, entered two new markets, and went through a difficult integration of three cultures into one.

As we wrapped up our dinner conversation, we couldn't help but reflect a bit on what just a couple of years before had seemed an impossible set of circumstances with which to contend. Now, having survived them and being able to look forward to a brighter business forecast ahead, it was a good time to stop and celebrate the accomplishment. It was also a good time to learn the lesson that needed to be learned. For Bob, the lesson was always to be prepared and not become complacent. Bob had this to say:

> It's hard to believe that we were so unprepared for the market downturn. We had let our guard down. We had become complacent and entitled. We took our business for granted. When it stopped coming in, it hit us like a hammer.

Bob's story emphasizes the problem with complacency and highlights the difference between management and leadership. When a business enjoys good economic conditions and success as Bob's did for fourteen years, management skills are needed to keep the business operating consistently and profitably. But when markets and conditions change, leadership skills are needed. Because Bob's firm lacked a leadership focus, they kept managing when they should have been leading. They should have been changing their strategies, developing new offerings, building skills, and taking their firm into new markets. Had they done so, it might have prevented the dramatic downsizing their company had to go through.

If your goal is to manage performance and maintain the status quo, you need management. If your goal is to change, improve, overcome, sell, or create something new, you need leadership. Bob's company actually needed both, as do most organizations. There are few management positions that require managing or leading exclusively. There are times to manage what you have and times to change what you have. Profitable operations need to be maintained, but they also need to be improved and adapted to changing conditions if they expect to remain profitable.

Depending on the situation, management can be just as important as leadership. The problem occurs when leadership skill is needed but only management skill is available. I worked for a manager once who had virtually no leadership skill. His focus was purely on accomplishing well-proven tasks and maintaining the status quo. He fostered no innovation, facilitated no new learning, and provided no inspiration or motivation. Regardless of the circumstance, he *managed* me. He told me what to do, how to do it, and when to do it. He didn't want my creative ideas. He didn't care about my need to contribute to the direction of the business or understand how to leverage my unique capabilities. His leadership approach was based purely on managing and controlling his people. It made my job miserable and drove me to find another one.

There are many subtle but important differences between people who function as managers and those who function as leaders. Managers think of their direct reports as subordinates; leaders think of their people as valuable assets. As popularized by Marcus Buckingham, author of *The One Thing You Need to Know*, managers focus on accomplishing what is necessary, while leaders focus on achieving what is possible. Management is maintaining; leading is creating.

Managing is about conformity, following policies, and maintaining consistency. Managing is about informing and reporting where leading is about motivating and inspiring. Managing is about maintaining budgets and resources. Leading is about creating new sources of revenue and implementing innovative approaches. Managing is about solving production problems where leading is about changing what gets produced. Leading is about changing direction and charting new courses.

Leadership guru Peter Drucker characterized a management mentality as *doing things right* versus a leadership mentality as *doing the right things*. Management emphasizes efficiency where leadership focuses on effectiveness. Managing involves reacting while leading involves being proactive. John C. Maxwell, author of *The 21 Irrefutable Laws of Leadership*, perhaps best characterizes the differences: he says that much of management involves tangibles where much of leading involves intangibles. The work of a leader involves softer skills and dealing with issues that are less visible. Leaders deal with the unknown, engage in the unseen, and create the future, while managers maintain the present.

Leading involves understanding and communicating the *why* in contrast to managing, which focuses on the *what* and enforcing the *how*. Managers are operationally focused, while leaders are focused on strategy and the bigger picture. Managers make operational improvements; leaders make business improvements. Managers implement initiatives; leaders conceive them. Managers follow agendas; leaders set them. Managers are like farmers; leaders are like hunters.

> LEADING IS NOT FOLLOWING THE WELL-WORN PATH OF THE HERD. LEADERSHIP IS CREATING A NEW PATH.

To sum up the differences, leaders *lead*. Leaders are out front. Leading is not following the well-worn path of the herd. Leadership is creating a new path. It is having the courage, taking the risk, stepping out, and persuading others to follow. It is creating momentum rather than managing it. Leading is an approach very different from managing, although both are important to an organization's success.

LEADERS VERSUS CONTRIBUTORS

As leading often involves the *why* of doing something and managing involves the *what*, the role of individual contributor in an organization is the one most involved in the *how*. Individual contributor work is the point where the proverbial rubber meets the road. It is the detailed *how-to* of the *what* that is behind the *why*.

All employees, regardless of title or level, are involved in some degree of individual contributor work. Even chief executives with multiple administrative assistants and large staffs make customer calls, create presentations, and perform other individual tasks. No one worthy of being called a great leader has the luxury of simply motivating, coaching, enabling, and directing others. They do some degree of *real work*, too.

Leading a team of people is not devoid of individual contributor work any more than it is devoid of management work. Leaders are involved in all three types of work: leading, managing, and doing. The key to being a great leader is having the right balance for the role and sphere of responsibility. If you manage five hundred people, fifty of whom are managers, the majority of your time and energy should be devoted to leadership activities. Your managers, particularly your first-line managers, are the ones who should be spending more of their time on management tasks. Your frontline employees in turn should be spending most of their time on individual contributor tasks. You *lead*, your managers *manage*, and your employees *do*. If, in contrast, you lead a small team of three people, you would perform the role of both leader and manager and also have responsibility for a substantive amount of individual contributor work.

Figure 1.1 depicts how your reliance on domain skills falls as your responsibility and sphere of influence increases. The more people you lead, the more you rely on leadership skills such as communications and coaching than you do on domain skills such as programming, engineering, or accounting. As you take on increasing levels of responsibility, the relative importance of leadership skills changes, too. What might have been the most important leadership skill to have at a lower level becomes less important at a higher level.

Figure 1.1: Skills Versus Sphere of Influence

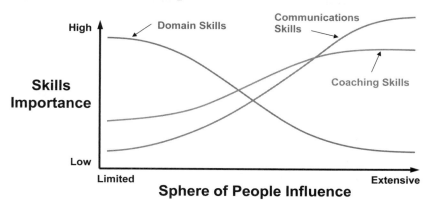

Everyone in a top-performing organization spends some amount of their time in each of the three areas of doing, managing, and leading. Even assemblers or clerks at the bottom of the organizational hierarchy have opportunities to apply management and leadership skills. They might help mentor a new hire, lead the implementation of a new procedure, or perform the quality assurance function for a colleague's work. It's just that leading and managing are much smaller parts of their job compared to someone more senior in the organization.

Leaders also need to maintain a degree of domain skill to remain relevant and effective coaches of their teams. Leaders need to stay current on domain vernacular, practices, and standards. The need for domain skill never goes completely away. It is the ratio of where leaders spend their time and energy that changes with their level of responsibility and influence.

As leaders take on more responsibility, they concern themselves more with their people's contributions and less with their own contributions. They subordinate much of their desire to do hands-on work to performing more strategic leadership duties. They work themselves out of their direct-contributing job. The highest compliment for great leaders is that they are working behind the scenes and their employees achieve their desired outcomes thinking they did it themselves.

For individual contributors who have a passion for hands-on work, moving into management can be frustrating. The transition into management requires doing less of the work they enjoyed as a direct contributor and doing more leading—a skill they have yet to develop and probably appreciate. Fortunately for them, most first-line management jobs include the need to be a coach to their team in the domain of the work they so enjoyed.

Effective leadership requires a balance of leadership, management, and individual contribution. For more senior executives in large companies, their time allocation percentage split between the three areas might be 60–30–10. A small-business owner who does a sizable amount of individual contributor work might have a split of 30–30–40.

Table 1.2 depicts some of the general differences in the role of a leader versus manager versus individual contributor to keep in mind when evaluating where you spend your time and where you should spend your time.

TABLE 1.2: DIFFERENCES BETWEEN LEADER, MANAGER, AND INDIVIDUAL CONTRIBUTOR ROLES			
	Contributor	**Manager**	**Leader**
	Focuses on the *how*	Focuses on the *how* and *what*	Focuses on the *what* and *why*
OBJECTIVE	Self-performance	Manage employee performance	Improve employee performance
SKILL FOCUS	Learning and developing own skills	Using people's skills	Developing people's skills
DIRECTION	Receives direction, executes the plan	Provides direction, creates the plan	Articulates the vision and strategy

	Contributor	Manager	Leader
RESPONSIBILITY	Domain tasks	Operations, tasks, quality	Strategy, people, culture, teamwork
CERTAINTY & RISK	Proven domain tasks, few risks	Proven management tasks, predictable results	Mostly intangibles, unknowns, ambiguities
TIME HORIZON	Short-term	Medium-term	Long-term
OVERALL FOCUS	Task completion, desired outcomes	Efficiency, quality, schedules, priorities	Effectiveness, relevance, positioning, growth
COMMUNICATION	Understands and acknowledges	Monitors, informs, and reports	Motivates, inspires, and coaches
TYPICAL METRICS	Individual output, contribution to team	Team's results, return on assets, cost containment	Overall results, profit, earnings, market share
IMPROVEMENTS	Identifies task improvements	Identifies process improvements	Identifies business improvements
INNOVATION	Stays within constraints	Manages constraints, maintains conformance	Stimulates creativity and innovation
INITIATIVES	Executes initiatives	Tracks and manages implementation of initiatives	Creates new initiatives and builds buy-in for them

	Contributor	Manager	Leader
RESOURCES	Works with resources as provided	Prioritizes and assigns resources	Identifies and secures resources as needed
FINANCIALS	Manages own budget, quota, expenses	Manages team expenses, quotas, budgets, forecasts	Oversees P/L, financial objectives, strategies
GUIDANCE	Guides self in use of procedures	Guides people on use of procedures, processes	Guides and coaches people on use of principles
VALUE-ADD	Direct	Indirect	Indirect and intangible

There are exceptions where individual contributors perform as much in the role of a leader as they do in the role of individual contributor. Sales is such a role. Because salespeople spend much of their time working with and influencing people, many of their responsibilities are similar to those of leaders. Many of the underlying competencies of great salespeople are the same as those of great leaders. As with great leaders, great salespeople motivate and inspire people to take action. Great salespeople think strategically and creatively. They secure resources and assimilate people into collaborative teams. They are proactive and action-oriented. They are influential. This is not to say that all salespeople make great leaders, but many do have the same qualities as great leaders. Those who become leaders significantly benefit from the competencies they developed in their sales experience.

CAPABILITY VERSUS TITLE

Some refer to leadership as a position with a title, such as executive vice president or general manager. Leadership, however, is not a function of position but a function of behavior. Leadership is not who you are but what you do. Leadership is about developing and employing the ability to achieve results through people. It is an internal ability, not a an external title or position. It is the skill of influencing people in order to achieve an intended result.

> LEADERSHIP IS NOT
> WHO YOU ARE BUT
> WHAT YOU DO.

Great leadership is not exercising positional power but rather the competencies of influence. It is a way of behaving, if not a way of life.

The SCOPE of Leadership framework is based on the competencies required to influence and deliver results through others. The competencies are used by successful leaders of large and small organizations alike. They apply equally well to anyone in a position of influence who seeks to produce results through people. They are competencies that motivate people to perform on their own instead of using authoritative power to coerce them to perform. Therefore, the SCOPE of Leadership book series is based on this definition of great leadership:

> **Great Leadership:** The ability to achieve a desired result through the influence of people who follow and perform by choice.

People follow great leaders because they choose to follow, not because they have to. People who follow by choice don't follow because they have to work in that job, are required by law, or must abide by the terms of a contract. That isn't a free choice to follow and doesn't reflect great leadership. You are not a leader unless people choose to follow you. If people follow you because of your position, you are a manager. Great leaders have followers because of their ability to influence, not because of their power and authority. Leadership is not an entitlement. Having people who follow by choice is a litmus test for great leadership.

The root of the word *leader* and *leadership* is *lead*. To be a leader requires that you lead people. It means you are out in front and people choose to follow you. It means you have a group of people you are taking somewhere. Leading isn't pushing from behind or controlling from the sidelines. It is assembling people, pulling them together, and leading them somewhere. It is reaching a desired destination with and through people.

People follow by choice because of the way their leaders exert influence. Great leaders are not coercive, commanding, or controlling. They are competent, collaborative, and encouraging. They are coaches, enablers, and motivators. They help people become better than people would be on their own. Great leaders improve people. They unselfishly serve, coach, and enable their constituents. They are leaders because what they do causes people to want to follow them.

People at all levels and in all roles can be leaders. Not only are managers, parents, preachers, maestros, and public company directors capable of being great leaders, but so are teachers, doctors, lawyers, receptionists, and bus drivers. A leader can be anyone in any position who influences customers, employees, audiences, relatives, investors, or citizens to do something to produce a desired result. The most successful communities, families, companies, and nonprofit organizations are those that have people thinking and behaving as leaders at all levels.

Organizations that scale, perform, lead their industries, and take care of their customers do so through *distributed leadership*. They have competent, responsible, influential people throughout the organization. Great organizations aren't great because of a single larger-than-life hero who is smarter, stronger, and better than everyone else. Great organizations rely on leadership throughout the organization—not just from a few people at the top.

Organization charts in high-performing organizations are almost meaningless because people at the very bottom of the hierarchy can be just as influential as people at the top. People at the bottom of high-performing organizations are just as involved as managers in solving customer complaints, coming up with new best practices, making important decisions, and leading in countless other ways. People at all levels are adept at coaching, enabling, encouraging, and leading others. They have the character, attitude, knowledge, and competence of a leader, just not the title. Leadership is more a matter of disposition than position.

> LEADERSHIP IS MORE A MATTER OF DISPOSITION THAN POSITION.

Leadership is a capability. To be precise, it is a competence more than a skill. Leadership is a broad aptitude and ability where a skill is often narrow and trade-specific. Skills can be short-lived, with some having a shelf life of just a few years. As industries, companies, fads, techniques, and technologies change, so do skills. Unlike domain skills, competencies—and in particular leadership competencies—transcend roles, titles, and trends.

MANAGEMENT VERSUS MASTERY

Organizations frequently promote people into management because they excelled in their domain, but when new managers attempt to use their domain expertise to lead their organization, they fail. They are often perceived by their employees as egotistical *supercontributors*, as they perform the work that their subordinates expect to be doing—and should be doing. New managers don't intend to fail; they simply want to be involved in the activities they have done before and have skill in. They want to be value-adding members of the team, but initially they know only how to add value through domain-related contributions.

Fortunately, most new managers figure out that their job is to develop the people on their team into the same superstars they were. For the managers who don't figure it out, they find themselves ousted from their management role, or their teams learn to work with them as contributors while another team member takes up the role of the leader.

As a coach, speaker, consultant, and trainer, I understand the satisfaction that comes with being a contributor. I enjoy the hands-on work I do. I enjoy *doing* as much as *leading*. The nature of doing in my field provides a lot of work diversity and enjoyable opportunities to engage with different individuals and organizations. Doing also gives me a valuable perspective and experience that continually enhances my abilities and the value I bring to my clients.

However, there are times when I miss the focus and satisfaction that come with leading a single organization. As a consultant and coach, I get to work closely with people, analyze issues, and conceive solutions, but I often miss out on implementation and experiencing the tangible results. There is not much more satisfying than experiencing the results of your work, which is the reason I enjoyed leading organizations for the first twenty years of my career.

I give you this perspective because my dual interest in performing hands-on work and leading others is not just my dichotomy. Most professionals aspire to take on more responsibility but also to be really good at something. People aspire to lead others but also to be experts. The problem people face, however, is that they can't be great leaders if they spend their time focused on their own work. To be great leaders, they have to devote themselves first to coaching, enabling, motivating, informing, and assimilating their people, leaving little time left for their own work.

If you find that your true interests are in doing rather than leading, don't force yourself into becoming a leader—at least not as a manager of people. There is a different career path available to you. Not everyone needs to have direct people responsibility. Choosing a career based on increasing domain competence as opposed to increasing people responsibility is a legitimate alternative. Having an expert level of skill still provides opportunities for you to have influence and responsibility, just not as measured by numbers of employees or layers of organizational responsibility.

Increased domain competence is a path that leads to mastery rather than management. Your opportunity to impact and influence others comes through your expertise in a domain rather than in leading and working through other people.

Since establishing my consulting and executive coaching company, my career choice has been to pursue mastery of a domain rather than management of people. My goal has been mastery of the domain of leadership. I don't want to take away from the value of leading and managing people, but to be fair to the great domain masters in the world, in many ways mastery is a greater challenge and reward.

As part of my pursuit of mastery, I've invested tens of thousands of hours learning, practicing, and performing. I've read hundreds of books and thousands of articles, and I've worked with thousands of people. I wake up as early as 4 a.m. to develop content and work on client projects. After working a full day, I read business books and psychology journals in the evenings. On days that I'm not speaking, leading a workshop, or consulting, I typically have a full schedule of coaching sessions with my coaching clients.

In all my consulting, coaching, and training engagements I request evaluative feedback, and when I receive criticism, I intensify my effort to improve and work on whatever I need to work on. Through it all, I've enjoyed the work and enabled many successes, but as a student who is constantly learning and striving to improve, it has been hard work. I've also made many mistakes. Reaching mastery is not a journey for the timid. It is a journey of constant learning, repeated engagement, receipt of feedback, and ongoing improvement. Mastery is a very challenging but also noble career.

If you are torn between pursuing more skill versus more people responsibility, consider either to be a respectable option. The world needs leaders of people as much as leaders of subject matter areas such as engineering, medicine, finance, and behavioral science. Mastery of a domain is just as much an accomplishment as being the CEO of a large organization. In the long term, it is often the masters, not the senior executives, who are most influential and remembered. Albert Einstein, Michelangelo, and Peter Drucker weren't fourth-line senior-level managers, yet they contributed more and left a more important legacy than most CEOs. Being a widely respected thought leader and sought-after expert is an honorable and satisfying position to attain.

You don't have to follow the typical management career path of increasing levels of people responsibility if it doesn't accommodate your true interests and passions. Leadership and influence through domain expertise and mastery can be just as rewarding, if not more so.

THE DEFINING CHARACTERISTIC

The real difference between leaders and others lies in how they effect change. Change requires breaking habits, thinking in new ways, and creating new behaviors. Leading people through change is very different from managing, doing, reacting, or following. Leading people through change is the ultimate test of a person's ability to lead and influence others. People who can effectively help others navigate through change, particularly through behavioral change, are true leaders and coaches.

> LEADING PEOPLE THROUGH CHANGE IS THE ULTIMATE TEST OF A PERSON'S ABILITY TO LEAD AND INFLUENCE OTHERS.

Many people who consider themselves good leaders when times are good discover they aren't as good as they thought when the economy falters. When their market share falls or their top customer defects, they realize they were managing when they thought they were leading. They should have changed their business model, enhanced their offerings, created a new strategy, obtained buy-in for a better approach, and developed the skills of their people. They discover they were great managers but not great leaders.

Leading people through change is the true mark of a leader. Persuading people to adopt a new program or work in a different way is not the same skill as maintaining the status quo. When you have the responsibility to revitalize a product, create a new market, or transform an underperforming organization, you are no longer managing. You are in a position that requires the ability to effect change. You are in a position that requires redirecting the organization's existing momentum into a new direction or creating a new source of momentum. This takes leadership, not management.

Managing an existing operation that is functioning relatively well requires maintaining standards of quality, ensuring compliance with procedures, holding people accountable for results, and making incremental improvements to processes, systems, and skills. Not an unimportant set of responsibilities, but compare these to what it takes to build a new organization or transform an existing one.

Transforming an underperforming operation requires changing roles, responsibilities, and people. It requires building new strategies, processes, and systems. It involves creating new products and services, acquiring new customers and developing new markets, and developing new attitudes, skills, and behaviors. It requires changing the organization's culture, traditions, and values. Leading change requires a set of skills and approaches that are much different from those needed to manage the status quo.

Effectively executing change requires a higher level of influence. You must inspire people to get out of their comfort zone; coach people through behavioral change; motivate people to embrace uncertainty, put in extra effort, and put themselves at risk; and help people deal with the frustrations of learning new skills, approaches, and systems. Great leadership includes the ability to effect change.

CAREER PROGRESSION

People don't generally become leaders without first working as individual contributors. In the management positions I held in my career, I certainly didn't, but not everyone follows a traditional career path. My progression to becoming an executive coach and leadership consultant certainly didn't. It wasn't when I was a child, when boys dream of being an astronaut or fireman, that I first aspired to be an executive coach.

As a quick review of my career and how I arrived where I am now: I left home and started working before finishing high school. I worked in several technical positions before becoming a junior engineer at Halliburton, putting myself through college, and receiving a bachelor's of science degree in engineering. A short time after graduating and starting a new job, about fifteen minutes to be exact, I found my interests were more related to business and people than technical analysis and design. It took a little more than another year, but I left my engineering career behind.

I joined IBM as a salesman, initially selling computerized engineering solutions. I then moved into general sales, then sales management, and then became a sales executive. Over my fifteen-year career with IBM, I worked in several divisions, held a variety of management positions, and built a reputation for turning around underperforming business units. I left IBM to join Scient, where I became one of their five global industry general managers. Scient was the fastest growing public company during the dot-com boom and the company that the industry used as a leading benchmark. Our company also became one of the fastest declining companies of all time during the dot-com bust. I took a short but refreshing sabbatical before joining LogicaCMG, where I was general manager of their North America financial services division.

Just before I turned forty-five years old, I went out on my own and launched my executive coaching and consulting company. I had no customers, no retainers, and no referrals. What I did have was experience in leading people, turning around underperforming businesses, and delivering results. As I promoted my new business venture and people became aware of my capabilities, my business started growing. At first, people hired me for business consulting, primarily related to sales performance improvement. Before long, however, I found myself spending more of my time helping and coaching individual executives. There are few business issues, including lagging sales, that are not rooted in people issues. To resolve the business issues I increasingly confronted, I started coaching and increasing my focus on behavioral science and leadership.

Over my career, I've been through three different stages that most leaders go through. In stage 1, I developed my domain skills. I worked in engineering and then in sales. In this first stage, I was an individual contributor and spent most of my time and energy applying the skills of my domain. From an overall career-building perspective, stage 1 could have been any domain such as accounting, writing, architecting, constructing, or banking. The important part of stage 1 was that I learned how to work, follow, and create value.

My second career stage started when I moved into sales management. When I became a manager, I initially tried leveraging my domain skills as most new managers do. I tried to be the *supercontributor*. It didn't work very well. Not only were there not enough hours in the day to be the team's primary contributor, but I also alienated my employees. I learned that I would need more than domain skills to be effective.

In this second stage, my focus shifted from domain expertise to business and management expertise. My technical knowledge of computing and engineering became less important. For stage 2 I needed business acumen. I focused on learning how to run my business unit. I developed my business management knowledge in areas like business planning and strategy formulation. I worked on learning brand promotion, marketing, and crafting partnerships. I focused on managing employee performance, hiring, and onboarding new employees.

During stage 2, I was fortunate to attend a number of management training programs, including IBM's management development program, a one-year advanced management program at Harvard Business School, and other programs taught by professors from many other prominent business schools. Between the ongoing education and the daily responsibilities of my management position, I turned away from my domain skills, exchanging them for business management skills.

In the third stage of my career, I turned my focus to people. I realized toward the end of my time with IBM and at the start of my work for Scient that the key to business performance was working with and through people. While I had obviously worked with people throughout my career up to that point, I didn't devote the majority of my time and energy to people. I had been more of a manager of a business than a leader of people.

In stage 3, I discovered that the highest levels of performance come through understanding how to work with and influence people. I maintained my interest and knowledge in running businesses, but I shifted my focus to understanding, developing, and leading people. I began to read books on leadership and study behavioral science. I attended leadership seminars and sought the counsel of successful people who were clearly effective leaders of people.

> I LEARNED THAT PEOPLE PRODUCE RESULTS, NOT SPREADSHEETS, REPORTS, POLICIES, PROCESSES, SYSTEMS, AND STRATEGIES.

Stage 3 was when I discovered that telling people what to do and focusing on results didn't produce optimal results. The more my people management responsibility increased, the more I realized the importance of motivating, inspiring, encouraging, coaching, facilitating, informing, enabling, and assimilating people. I learned that people produce results, not spreadsheets, reports, policies, processes, systems, and strategies. Having the right strategy and infrastructure in place are important, but they don't create results. People do.

Focusing on people is still what I do today. Coaching, enabling, and effecting change in people is the most personally and professionally rewarding stage of my career yet. My only regret is that I didn't transition into stage 3 earlier in my career. Had I realized the degree of achievement that comes through people rather than projects, tasks, business plans, and assets, I could have been more effective much earlier.

During the move into each new stage in my career, I inevitably lost some competence I had developed in the prior stage as I turned my attention to developing new competencies. I made an objective, however, to retain as much of my prior knowledge and skill as possible. Leading people doesn't remove the value of understanding the details of how your organization operates.

If you think becoming a leader means you concern yourself only with the big picture, think again. Leading organizational change requires a broad set of capabilities. Great leadership requires being able to relate to people on many levels. Much of my own success is as much due to my knowledge of leadership as it is to my knowledge of other domains I've developed and kept up with. I regularly utilize not only my knowledge of sales and psychology, for example, but also the analytical and design skills I learned early in my career as an engineer. I also continue to look for opportunities to engage in diverse new activities and learn new skills. Regardless of your position, if you expect to increase your contribution and relevance continually, there is tremendous value in building and maintaining as much knowledge as you can.

There was also a stage 0 in my career. This stage was the time I spent working on my college education and developing my initial domain skills. Because I worked full-time while going to college, my stage 0 and stage 1 happened concurrently.

Most of the successful veteran executives I work with characterize their career in these four stages. These same four stages are the basis of a career-stage framework developed by consulting group Novations, which they call the Four Stages of Contribution model. It reflects the four stages of increasing impact a person's contributions have as they take on more responsibility and exert more influence. The stages are expressed in mathematical formulas as shown inTable 1.3.

TABLE 1.3: THE FOUR STAGES OF CAREER CONTRIBUTION

1. **Dependent Contribution:** Dependent contribution is the *learning* stage, where your value (V) equals your contribution (Y) divided by the number of others (n) helping you deliver your contribution. The formula for dependent contribution is $V = Y / n$. In other words, the more help you require from others in order to perform your work, the lower the net value that you produce.

2. **Independent Contribution:** Independent contribution is the *domain expertise* stage, where your value equals your contribution. The formula for independent contribution is $V = Y$. When you become a self-sufficient individual contributor, your direct contribution equals the value you produce.

3. **Contributing through Others:** Contributing through others is the *local leadership* stage, where your value equals your contribution multiplied by the number of people (n) within your direct sphere of influence. The formula for contributing through others is $V = Y \times n$. The more people you positively influence, the more value you produce. Studies find that over 80 percent of people who contribute through local leadership are not in management positions.

4. **Contributing Strategically:** Contributing strategically is the *shaping the organization* stage, where your value equals your contribution raised to the power of the number of people your contribution influences. The formula for strategic contribution is $V = Y^n$. This represents the exponential effect of leadership. Your direct influence impacts people, who in turn impact other people, who impact other people. Contributing strategically means your influence is no longer localized to the people you work with directly. Your influence is extended across geographies, industries, families, and generations. Studies find that 65 percent of those who contribute strategically are not in management positions. They are masters of competencies and knowledge who influence others through their thought leadership.

As you grow in your career and increase your influence, you increase the value you contribute. Your contribution can be through a domain skill, in a management position, or as a leader who influences others from any position. Leadership is based on the extent your contributions and influence cause others to create value and reach desired outcomes.

Career Growth and the Necessity to Learn

There are three implications that go with increasing responsibility. The first is the decreasing emphasis on domain skills. You spend less time in domain areas like selling, engineering, and programming as you take on more responsibility leading, coaching, motivating, informing, and assimilating people. You focus less on tasks and more on people. Your domain skills give way to general and interpersonal skills.

The second implication of taking on increased levels of responsibility is that you often feel you are taking a step backward. When you change your career or take on a new responsibility, you enter a new learning curve. There are new skills to develop, knowledge to acquire, and relationships to build. There may be new customers to meet, jargon to grasp, products to learn, and markets to understand.

The realization that you have so much to learn can feel overwhelming. It makes you feel as if you are regressing at first. You feel a sense of incompetence and insecurity as you let go of your time-tested old skills to start building new ones. Before you felt like a veteran professional; now you feel like an amateur.

It is tempting to think you should know everything as you gain higher levels of responsibility, but the opposite is closer to the truth. Taking on more responsibility sometimes means you start out knowing very little. Great leaders whose advancements take them into new industries, new markets, or new countries often feel as if they are starting all over again. To take on more responsibility requires that you continually learn.

The third implication of taking on more responsibility is that at some point you will rise to the challenge. You will learn how to handle the higher-level responsibility and settle in. When you settle in, your learning will slow down, and you will feel as though you've stalled. When you move past the early gains of learning and the rate of learning slows, you'll feel disappointment. It's like achieving any goal that causes you to lose something in exchange—the hope, anticipation, and challenge that had been pushing you.

As depicted in Figure 1.2, when you experience a career plateau, you have four choices. You can advance your career in a new domain and start the learning process over; you can advance your career by pursuing additional responsibility in your current domain; you can push through the learning plateau to move from being competent in a domain to being a master in it; or lastly, you can stop growing, settle in, and get comfortable.

Figure 1.2: Career and Skill Progression

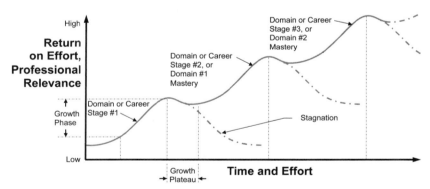

If you choose the fourth option and become comfortable, expect to start the process of stagnation and losing your professional relevance. Choosing to settle in and become comfortable can work for a short while, but it isn't sustainable. When you stagnate, you lose effectiveness. You ultimately become obsolete and irrelevant. The necessary pain of leadership, as with any other knowledge-based role, is that you must keep learning and growing.

Nothing stays the same or lives forever. Of the one hundred largest United States companies in the early twentieth century, fewer than fifteen remained at the beginning of the twenty-first century. Nothing stands still, especially within a broad responsibility such as leadership.

Where are you on the skill and career progression curve? Are you still growing or are you stagnating? If you expect to stay relevant, effective, and employed, continue to learn and grow. Continue to take on more responsibility or learn and develop in your domain. Develop at a level equal to or greater than that of your industry, domain, and responsibility. Otherwise you will fall behind.

You may not want to make the learning investment required to become a great leader, but realize that you have to make an investment in something if you want to remain relevant. Learning is a necessity in any professional role. The question you should consider is not whether to learn but what to learn. If you choose to make leadership your learning subject, the added benefit is that you build competencies you can use in any domain, industry, or role. You use leadership competencies both professionally and personally. Leadership development is one of the best learning investments you can make.

A DIFFERENT VIEW OF ADVERSITY

People generally pursue prosperity and avoid adversity, but ironically adversity helps people accomplish their goals and achieve prosperity. People who have been through adversity are far more knowledgeable and experienced than those who have not. Adversity causes people to grow and learn. It teaches, refines, and develops people. Adversity produces competence, perseverance, character, and gratitude—all qualities possessed by great leaders.

How do you see adversity? Do you see a hardship as something to avoid or something to embrace? Do you let adverse circumstances get you down, or do you appreciate them? While not as enjoyable as prosperity, adversity provides a tremendous developmental benefit. In contrast, prosperity provides little developmental benefit. Prosperity rarely develops the best in people—it merely covers up the worst.

> PROSPERITY RARELY DEVELOPS THE BEST IN PEOPLE—IT MERELY COVERS UP THE WORST.

Great leaders have typically been through a lot of adversity. They have been through bankruptcy or been close to it. They have been fired or laid off. They have dealt with physical health issues. They've been in circumstances that denied them comforts and conveniences others take for granted. They've had to personally pay for their mistakes and poor judgment. Yet through their trials, they learned lessons that honed their skills and made them better leaders.

People who obtain their education, belongings, and opportunities without much difficulty miss out on valuable learning and growth. They are like children who lack context, appreciation, and understanding for what most adults contend with. People who have only seen prosperity are ill-prepared to contend with personnel issues, the demands of competitive markets, and the stress of work. They are not prepared for leadership.

There are also people who encounter adversity but are no better off than those who don't because they neglect to learn from it. Instead of leveraging the opportunity to learn, they react to their adversity by blaming others, blaming circumstances, or seeing themselves as victims. Instead of growing and benefiting from their adversity, they sulk in it.

The growth that adversity produces in great leaders isn't related as much to their specific hardship as it is to how they learn to react to it. Great leaders learn to react to adversity constructively. They even get to the point that they value and embrace it. They see adversity as an opportunity to be capitalized on, rather than a hopeless situation to be discouraged by.

There is plenty of adversity around, including many people's discouraging behavior and negative sentiment. There are incompetent bosses, selfish coworkers, complaining neighbors, and disgruntled customers. There are family difficulties, relationship problems, financial challenges, and health complications. Life is filled with problems, challenges, conflict, and complexity. It seems, too, that life inevitably gets more complex and difficult for many people. Unfortunately, it causes people to run from adversity and take refuge in comforts and conveniences that are not conducive to learning and growing. Paradoxically for many people, the more they pursue prosperity and seek to be comfortable, the more discomfort they encounter and adversity they create. There really is no escaping adversity, so when it comes along, you might as well learn from it.

To use adversity to your advantage, accept it. Don't go out of your way to create it, but when it comes, consider yourself fortunate to have it. Leverage it instead of getting mad at it, becoming depressed over it, or running from it. Ask yourself how you and your team can benefit from it. Learn and gain knowledge from your frustrating circumstances. Improving yourself is much more fun and beneficial than feeling defeated. Use your adversity to be a better person and leader. The greater your struggle, the greater your reward will be.

Some of today's best public speakers are those who had to overcome a fear of public speaking. Some of the world's richest people started with absolutely nothing. Thomas Edison had many failures. He tried unsuccessfully to extract iron from ore in the 1880s. He couldn't convince people to buy a new concoction of his called "cement." He was a poor student. When a schoolmaster called him "addled," his furious mother took him out of school and taught him at home.

German composer and pianist Ludwig van Beethoven's music teacher once told him that he was hopeless as a composer. Winston Churchill failed the sixth grade. John Creasy, the English novelist who wrote 564 books, had his manuscripts rejected 753 times before he became established.

German physicist Albert Einstein was four years old before he spoke, and he spoke with confusing pauses until he was nine. He was advised to drop out of high school as his teachers told him he would never amount to much. One headmaster expelled him from school. He even failed several sections of his entrance exam into college.

Influential Dutch artist Vincent van Gogh failed as an art dealer, flunked his entrance exam to theology school, and was fired by the church after an ill-fated attempt at missionary work. During his life, he seldom experienced anything other than failure as an artist. Although a single painting by van Gogh would ultimately fetch in excess of $100 million, in his lifetime he sold only one of his paintings, four months prior to his death.

Technologists Bill Hewlett and Dave Packard's early failed products included a lettuce-picking machine and an electric weight-loss machine. Prior to founding Microsoft, Paul Allen and Bill Gates designed a computerized system for municipal traffic management called Traf-O-Data that never sold. American automotive pioneer Henry Ford's first two automobile businesses failed. Michael Jordan was cut from his high school basketball team. President Abraham Lincoln lost more races than he won—he lost a local legislative race, three congressional races, and two senatorial races, and failed at an attempt to become vice president.

I share all this with you for two reasons. First, if you are in adverse circumstances or lack a competence, don't let it stop you from pursuing leadership. Great leaders become great through the honing and development that come with adversity. You can rise above whatever you may be dealing with. Don't let adversity keep you down any more than it kept down Henry Ford, Bill Gates, or Albert Einstein. Use the resistance, obstacles, embarrassments, and mistakes in your life to get motivated; don't relegate yourself to being a victim. Adversity is like the unwelcome particle that irritates the oyster but in doing so creates the stunning pearl. It is the process an ugly caterpillar goes through to become a beautiful butterfly. Don't waste the adversity in your life. Leverage it. Let it help you become a better leader.

> ADVERSITY IS LIKE THE UNWELCOME PARTICLE THAT IRRITATES THE OYSTER BUT IN DOING SO CREATES THE STUNNING PEARL.

Second, if you are prosperous and have been for some time, your comfortable circumstances may be more of a disadvantage to you than an advantage. It's probably time to become uncomfortable. Challenge yourself and your team to start growing, learning, and improving again. Choose to become a better leader even if you have attained a senior executive position and are sipping lattes in your swiveling, reclining, ergonomically designed desk chair in your mahogany-veneered corner office. Create some cognitive dissonance. Challenge your thinking. Get out of your comfort zone. Learn how to become an even better leader.

THE PROBLEM WITH POWER

Having power, as leaders usually do, is akin to having prosperity. It provides as much of a disadvantage as it does an advantage. While having more authority and power is a career aspiration for many people, those who gain it are often made worse by it. As with prosperity and success, power has a negative side effect.

When people gain authority over other people, the power they gain causes them to see people and situations differently. When many people obtain power, their elevated status causes them to become egocentric. They feel more exclusive and become more likely to see others as less important. Their self-centeredness is further amplified as other people react to their power with fear, intimidation, and admiration.

Without a conscious effort to stay grounded in moral values and maintain a focus on the good of the whole team, people in positions of power lose their empathy. They lose the ability to see situations as others do. They become overly optimistic, thinking that there is less risk than there truly is and that they have more control over events than they really do. They become overly confident and aggressive, thinking they are better than they really are. Some take it to the extreme of thinking of themselves as being above the law, above company policy, and above ethical standards.

Power comes not only through higher levels of authority but also through fame and fortune. The challenge for people in senior positions of authority is that they are often subject to all three. For some, the combination is lethal. They can't handle it. For great leaders, though, money, power, and status aren't deterrents. Great leaders don't let their elevated authority, status, and financial means separate them from reality. They remain grounded in the core values and competencies of great leadership. They don't let prosperity and power lessen their ability to learn, relate, and lead.

Be assured that you don't need to be an egocentric, selfish, uncaring person to be a leader. Great leaders are powerful and often wealthy, but they are not selfish. They don't abuse their power and status. They don't let it get to their heads. They use their power for the good of their organization, not themselves. They use their resources as much for their family, community, and charitable causes as for themselves.

FOLLOWERSHIP

Leading also involves following, just as following involves leading. Early adopters—those who are quick to adopt and follow someone else—are also leaders. They might not be *the* leader, but being an early follower requires leadership qualities such as courage and confidence. A first follower is just one step away from being the leader. They are in stark contrast to the stereotypical followers who wait to give their support to something after everyone else already has. Followers, particularly early followers, are leaders themselves. They lead other people to follow them.

Followers also become leaders when in situations void of leadership. When they work for bosses who don't lead, employees rise up to become the true leaders. Community citizens who speak up and take action when their community leaders, schools, and governments don't lead as they should become the true leaders.

Leaders are also followers. When choosing to become a great leader, expect to lead, but don't always expect to be the one at the top or out front. Great leaders are also great followers. There are few leaders who don't have bosses, boards, customers, investors, or other stakeholders they have to follow. Everyone, including a great leader, is in a role that requires following others. Leadership involves both leading and following.

As a leader, you also follow the people before you. If you took over an existing organization, you joined something that others created. You followed the work of others. There were people before you who developed and maintained the organization that provided you with the opportunity to become a part of it. So, too, will others come after you, assuming you continue to develop and maintain the organization in a way that provides them a similar future opportunity. Even if you started your own company, there were others who performed similar work before you that you learned and benefited from.

The principles of leadership used by great leaders involve followership. Loyalty, humility, stewardship, learning, and listening, for example, are qualities of great leaders as much as they are of great followers. Becoming a great leader means you also become a great follower.

Counterintuitively, followers are just as important to leaders as leaders are to followers. Leaders are indebted to their followers. If it weren't for followers, leaders wouldn't be leaders. Managers don't have jobs if they don't have employees. Politicians aren't elected if people don't vote for them. The hard work and support of people enables leaders to lead. Great leaders are grateful for their privilege and opportunity to have followers. They give their followers their utmost admiration and respect. Followers are grateful as well for leaders who demonstrate great leadership.

> LEADERS ARE INDEBTED TO THEIR FOLLOWERS. IF IT WEREN'T FOR FOLLOWERS, LEADERS WOULDN'T BE LEADERS.

Leaders and followers have a symbiotic relationship. It is not a matter of the leader being better or more important than the follower. In high-performing organizations, leaders and followers support and enable one another equally. Both roles are vitally important and sometimes interchangeable.

THE RESPONSIBILITY

Leadership doesn't exist without followers, which means leadership is not as much about the leader as it is about the team being led. Being in a position of leadership requires focusing on others. It comes with a responsibility to care for people. Having followers is a tremendous honor, but it also represents a duty.

Having followers is a reflection of your wisdom, experience, talent, and stewardship. It recognizes your positive influence and validates that you provide something worth following. It is a reward for capably dealing with adversity, overcoming obstacles, and rising to the many challenges that organizations face. Being a great leader means you've invested time, energy, and money into developing yourself and your ability to lead. You've learned how to coach, encourage, and improve people. You've frequently put the interests of others ahead of your own. You've made the sacrifice that leadership requires.

People leadership is not like managing a project, monitoring the quality of a process, or producing a product. What you do impacts people, families, and livelihoods. You impact organizations, customers, suppliers, and stockholders. The decisions and actions you influence can lead to catastrophic failure or incredible success for many people. Whether you lead an organization, family, or community, being the leader means you have a significant responsibility.

If you don't want to be responsible, don't accept a position of responsibility. If you don't want to care for people, don't aspire to move into management. You are not ready. Leadership is a people job that carries a sizable responsibility. If you are up to the task, however, leadership is extremely rewarding. There is little more satisfying than helping people become the best they can be. Choose to be a leader.

PRINCIPLES IN REVIEW

Here are key principles from this chapter to keep in mind.

- **Leadership:** Leadership is the ability to achieve a desired result through the influence of people who perform and follow by choice.
- **Contribution:** Everyone provides *leading, managing*, and *doing* contributions regardless of position or title.
- **Mastery:** Expertise and domain mastery are just as effective platforms for influence as being in a people management position.
- **The Leadership Test:** Leading people through change, in particular behavioral change, is the ultimate test of a person's ability to lead and influence others.
- **Adversity:** Learn and grow through your adversity rather than let it get you down.
- **Prosperity and Power:** When in prosperous times and positions of power, resist the temptation to become

comfortable and self-centered. Continually strive to learn, improve, and stay grounded in moral values.

- **Responsibility:** Don't accept a position of responsibility if you don't want to take responsibility.

CHAPTER THREE

LEARNING TO LEAD

If your actions inspire others to dream more, learn more, do more, and become more, you are a leader.

—**John Quincy Adams**

Twentieth-century quality-control pioneer W. Edwards Deming found that 94 percent of business performance problems were attributable to systems, processes, and strategies. Only 6 percent were attributable to the performance of employees. Jeff Juran, another well-regarded authority on quality and author of *The Quality Control Handbook*, claimed that 85 percent of organizational performance problems were attributable to causes other than the employee.

These findings have moved many managers to focus on systems, processes, and strategic planning. Their thinking is that if they execute a well-crafted strategy through people in well-defined roles with well-aligned systems and well-designed processes, they will obtain productive employees, quality products, and well-performing organizations. This is a logical approach—to a point. The point at which it breaks down is when managers take it to the extreme, making their processes, systems, measurements, and strategies more important than their people. When managers make people the conforming or expendable part of the organizational ecosystem, they are creating as many problems as they might think they are solving.

There are two significant issues managers create when they promote a management approach that isn't centered on people. First, with the exception of only the most repetitive of production-oriented tasks, a rigid *plug and play* system underleverages people's capabilities. A system in which people are plugged into highly scripted processes uses only a fraction of their ability and even less of their knowledge.

Processes and systems should enable people, not turn them into robots. Using processes and systems strictly to control people is like restaurant managers mandating their waitstaff follow scripts verbatim rather than allowing them to personalize their customer conversations. The result is a customer experience that makes customers feel processed rather than personalized. It is like car salespeople who are required to follow structured sales systems. When you leave their car dealership, you feel like you just went through a mechanical process and wonder if you received information that was right for you, much less the truth. Neither the waitstaff nor the salespeople were able to use their true abilities, nor were the customers given the best service.

The second issue is that people want a degree of flexibility and independence. People don't like being controlled like robots. They want to use their mind and abilities. They want to use their unique experiences, education, and talents. For people to be fully engaged, feel passionate about their work, and give their best effort, they need to feel they are more than machines in a production operation.

Processes, systems, strategies, role definitions, and measurements are critical to an organization's success, but they shouldn't come before people. They are not substitutes for leadership. As much as some managers might believe that performance is all about managing an organization's infrastructure, no manager can deny that most every competitive, differentiating organizational quality is the result of people. People conceive great new products, launch compelling marketing programs, produce differentiated strategies, and provide excellent customer service. In managers' defense, modifying a process or system can be easier than modifying a person's thinking, but that doesn't make it more effective.

Even Deming, the systems and process expert, turned his attention to people. He surprised many of his followers when he began to advocate management principles over quality principles. In his book, *Out of the Crisis,* he presented fourteen points of management that addressed improving business effectiveness, primarily by working through people. The key principles he advocated involved developing skills, promoting cooperation, gaining trust, finding joy in work, securing a sense of ownership, and having strong *leadership*. He promoted the idea that companies should substitute leadership for numerical quotas, annual rating systems, management by objectives, and the use of fear as an approach to motivate desired behaviors.

Creating and sustaining high-performance organizations requires a focus on people. Processes and systems should be designed to enable people rather than control them.

> PROCESSES AND SYSTEMS SHOULD BE DESIGNED TO ENABLE PEOPLE RATHER THAN CONTROL THEM.

Reaching top levels of performance requires leaders who know how to produce results through people's unique abilities. Learning leadership is therefore primarily about learning the competencies that enable people to perform. It is learning how to coach, exhort, enable, inform, and assimilate people.

THE GENETICS OF LEADERSHIP

Behavioral science finds that we are products of both nature and nurture. Our fundamental genetic makeup is activated or left dormant because of our environmental influences. Not only our genes but also the experiences we have, relationships we maintain, education we receive, and circumstances we encounter significantly influence who we become. They collectively determine who we are.

With few exceptions, other than how we look, very little of what we do or become is the sole result of our genes. Even our height is not 100 percent inherited. Studies find that 5 to 30 percent of our height is attributable to environmental factors, as is 50 to 80 percent of our personality and 20 to 50 percent of our intelligence. What we do—including what we eat—has a significant impact on our physical characteristics. As with most behavioral characteristics, leadership is not the product of a gene. Leadership competence is learned and developed.

Neuroscience finds that competencies are networks of brain cells connected through thousands of synaptic connections. The reason one person gives a more compelling presentation than another is that they spent more time and energy developing the patterns of synaptic connections in their brains that produce their presentation competence.

Your competencies, attitudes, and behaviors are the products of both your physical makeup and your environmental influences. Your emotions, thinking, physical habits, values, experiences, and genetic predispositions all play a role in what you choose to do and how you do it. The outcomes you produce can be traced back through a number of elements that contain both conscious and unconscious thought. The outcomes you aspire to produce in the future can also be modified through changes in the same elements. One of the most frequent questions I receive from executives is if their efforts in coaching their people can actually make a difference. They want to know if people can actually change their behavior. My answer is always an absolute yes.

The results that people produce are created by a chain of events. A sustainable *result* is the product of a *habit*. A habit is the product of a *behavior*. A behavior is the outcome of a *mindset*. A mindset is the by-product of a *thought*. A thought is created by a thought-provoking external event or an inner drive, or *purpose*. A purpose comes from long-held guiding *principles* based on deep subconscious *values and beliefs*. Deeply held unconscious beliefs are based on the interaction of our *genes* with our *environmental influences*.

This continuum between genetics and results reveals four levels of change that you and those whom you influence make. The first level of change involves what you do. It is based on your behavior and actions. It is the easiest level of change to undertake and simply involves changing how you do something, such as taking a different route to work or implementing a biweekly versus monthly staff meeting.

The second level of change involves what you consciously think. It is based on the conscious decisions you make, which drive your behaviors. It is the conscious mindset that causes you to do what you do. This requires a slightly more difficult level of change, such as changing the goals and strategies you set that drive the decisions you make, changing how you think about your work or how you react to people who upset you, or changing a negative outlook into a positive one.

The third level of change involves your unconscious thought. It is based on the deeply held beliefs and guiding principles that unconsciously drive your thinking. Changing your unconscious thought is possible but is a more difficult level of change. It requires that you bring your deep-rooted instincts and principles into your consciousness and involves becoming aware of the biases, beliefs, and values that drive your thinking. This level of change could involve changing how you perceive cultures, politics, or religion or changing parts of your well-developed identity and personality.

The fourth level of change involves your surroundings and circumstances. It is based on the people you spend time with, the situations you put yourself into, and the level of nurturing you receive. It could involve changes to engrained habits that change not only your physical routines but also your physiology. These influences determine how your genes express themselves. You could have a natural gift for art, but if you are never in a situation that requires your artistic ability, your artistic gifts never have a chance to express themselves. Changing your physiology and surroundings is the most difficult level of change; changes at this level can involve competing with your body's physical addictions, cravings, and hormone fluctuations. It can require ending relationships, creating new relationships, relocating physically, changing roles, or embarking on a new career path.

You have control over elements impacting all four of these levels of change, and you make choices at all four levels that can be altered. The example below shows how the effects of these elements can build on your genetic foundation through a chain of ten events that work together to produce a certain result.

Genetic Expression (Level 4 Change):

1. **Genes and nurturing**—Your DNA and RNA combine with your childhood experience of playing math games and growing up on a steady diet of wild salmon, cacao beans, and green tea.

2. **Gene expression**—You develop a left-brain logical orientation and attend engineering school, which brings out your aptitude for analytical thinking.

Unconscious Thought, Deeply Held Values, and Instincts (Level 3 Change):

3. **Belief**—Based on your early nurturing, education, and aptitudes, you develop a belief that value in society is created through technological improvements.

4. **Principle**—You unconsciously live and work by a guiding principle that you can best solve problems through the application of technology.

Conscious Thought (Level 2 Change):

5. **Goal**—A new opportunity comes along at work that you become passionate about, and you set a goal to develop an industry-leading technology.

6. **Thought**—To accomplish your goal, you conceive a plan that includes meeting with investors and potential suppliers to help develop the new technology.

7. **Attitude**—As you prepare for your meetings, you develop feelings of excitement, as well as anxiety, both of which combine to create an entrepreneurial mindset. You consciously develop a *positive can-do* attitude.

Behaviors (Level 1 Change):

8. **Behavior**—Seemingly out of character for you, you buy a new suit, shave off your beard, and show up in the office one day with an aura of confidence and looking as if you've been through a makeover.

9. **Habit**—People's compliments reinforce your new image and cause you to create a habit of looking clean, neat, and professional that continues after your supplier and investor meetings.

10. **Results**—Your habit of looking sharp and exuding confidence results in your being viewed more positively by upper management, which ultimately gives you the opportunity to take on a leadership position in the engineering department.

Any one of these ten behavior-influencing elements as depicted in Figure 1.3 could have been the determining factor that ultimately created your leadership opportunity. It could have been your early nurturing as much as your education, beliefs, goals, thoughts, attitudes, or behaviors. In reality, it was all of these combined. It was the result of many influences, decisions, and experiences.

Figure 1.3: Genetics to Results—Four Levels of Change

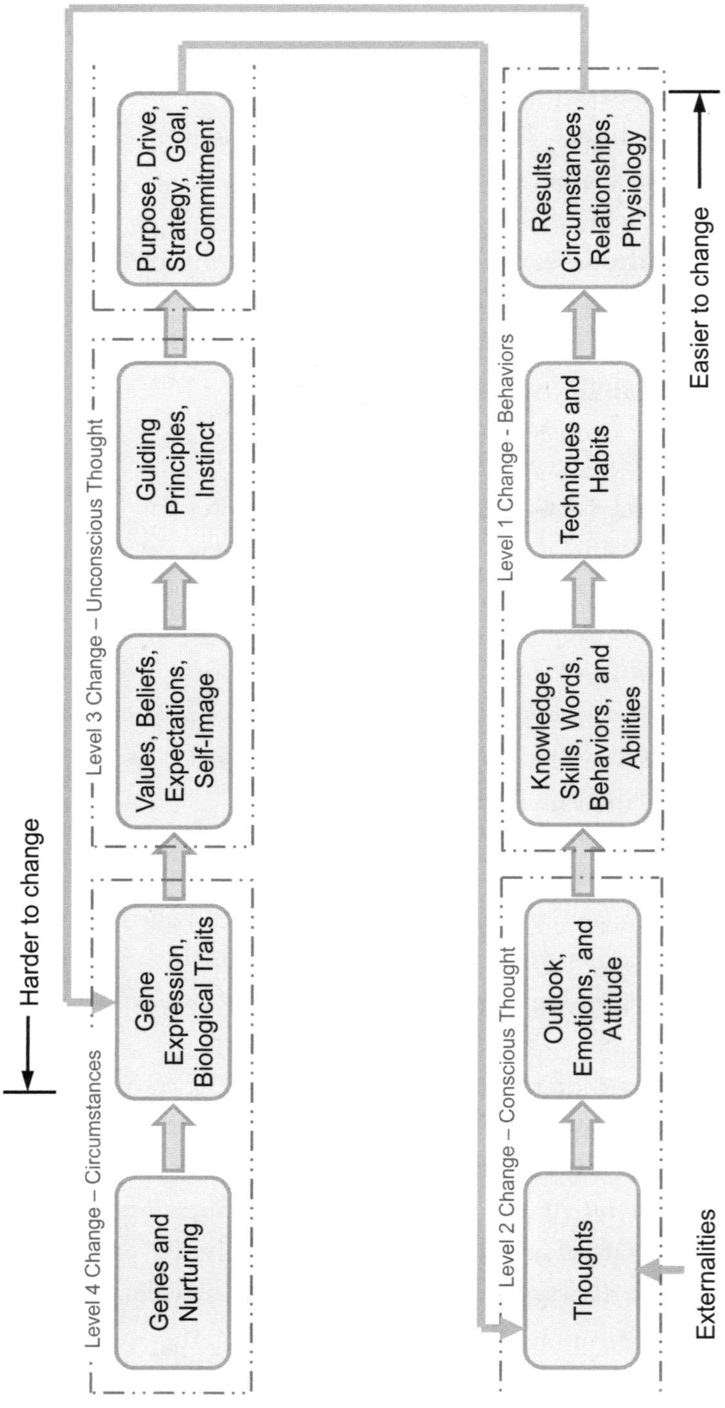

Harder to change

Easier to change

Externalities

Level 4 Change – Circumstances

Genes and Nurturing

Gene Expression, Biological Traits

Level 3 Change – Unconscious Thought

Values, Beliefs, Expectations, Self-Image

Guiding Principles, Instinct

Purpose, Drive, Strategy, Goal, Commitment

Level 2 Change – Conscious Thought

Thoughts

Outlook, Emotions, and Attitude

Level 1 Change – Behaviors

Knowledge, Skills, Words, Behaviors, and Abilities

Techniques and Habits

Results, Circumstances, Relationships, Physiology

This example shows that leadership is not the result of having the right parents any more than it is going to a certain school, developing a certain attitude, or learning a specific skill. Leadership, like most behaviors, is a learned and developed capability. Your thoughts, decisions, and actions determine your leadership ability. You gain knowledge, put it into practice, build experience, and repeat the process. You read books, seek wise counsel, and apply yourself. Leadership competence is a result of everything about you—your genes, nurturing, knowledge, and experience.

As a coach, you help other people learn, grow, and change. You help other people improve their skills and change their behaviors. You confront a wide variety of issues that emanate from all four of these levels of change. Both coaching and learning to lead involves changing behaviors, thoughts, beliefs, and circumstances.

If you are a golf coach, for example, you have students who need only a *level 1 change* in their behavior, such as how to grip their clubs. You simply show them the correct grip, and they relatively easily make the change.

You also encounter students needing a *level 2 change* in their thinking, such as knowing which club to select. You help them change their conscious thinking by creating an understanding in them about which club is most appropriate to use in a given situation.

Students needing a *level 3 change* in their subconscious thinking might include learning the source of their anger when they miss a putt. You help them become aware of the subconscious thoughts driving their anger and help them develop new patterns of unconscious thought that enable them to control their anger.

You encounter students needing a *level 4 change* when you determine their need to find a different interest area. They might be addicted to golf, yet be so bad at it and upset when they play that they really need to find a new interest. You help them find their new interest and the resources they need to get settled into it.

People can change regardless of the level of change they may need to confront. You were not a born leader, nor was anyone else—

nor was anyone born anything else. People are the result of change. They are the result of both nature and nurture. They are the result of nurturing, learning, development, coaching, and encouragement.

STRENGTHS VERSUS WEAKNESSES

Great leaders utilize their strengths and those of their people, but learning leadership isn't merely about enhancing existing capabilities. Learning leadership is about building a set of competencies that can be called into action as situations require them. Leadership competence is like a craftsman's tool belt containing a variety of tools, each designed for a different purpose.

In contrast, relying on a few dominant strengths is like having a tool belt with only a few tools or only one tool. For some managers, their primary tool is a big hammer. It is a powerful tool, able to crush most anything, but its strength is insufficient and inappropriate for effectively dealing with every situation that comes along. A manager's hammer is a poor substitute for a situation that requires a wrench or a screwdriver. The problem with relying on only a few strengths is that you often use the wrong tool in situations that would be better handled with a different tool.

Great leaders have a rich tool belt that enables them to use the right tool for the right situation. They have a hammer but also a sharp scalpel, mirror, flashlight, drill, file, and other tools needed to perform the work they have to perform. They can adeptly handle most any situation because they have the right tools in their tool belt.

Another problem with relying too much on a few strengths is that they not only can be the wrong tools for a given situation but also can be overapplied even in the right situation. Overused strengths are as inappropriate as those used in the wrong situation. They produce unintended and often unfortunate consequences. Strengths overused, as with strengths used inappropriately, are actually weaknesses.

For example, an extremely technical person who is considered an expert on a given topic might lack the ability to communicate effectively to businesspeople at a business level. When in a business setting, his strength of being able to understand technical details becomes a weakness. He would be more effective if he had an ability to get out of the technical details and talk at a business level. Using a strengths-based philosophy, he

> STRENGTHS OVERUSED, AS WITH STRENGTHS USED INAPPROPRIATELY, ARE ACTUALLY WEAKNESSES.

might only continue to enhance his technical strength, causing him to neglect other abilities that would make him more effective. With just a little coaching and practice, he could add the tool of effective communications to his tool belt and be significantly more capable and helpful to his organization.

There are countless examples of overused strengths that become weaknesses. Managers who excel at encouraging and uplifting others often have trouble confronting conflict and holding people accountable. Their strength at being encouragers works against them when they need to be assertive. If they develop the ability to be constructively assertive in addition to being positive and encouraging, they gain a tool that makes them much more effective leaders. Alternatively, managers who are especially adept at holding their people accountable and being candid have trouble being an encourager. If they develop their empathy and ability to relate to people, they gain a tool that makes them more effective leaders.

People's strengths often reveal their weaknesses because people tend to overuse their strengths and cause a corresponding weakness It is easy to recognize when you look for it or analyze people's 360 assessment survey results. In my company's SCOPE of Leadership 360 leadership competency assessment, we can generally predict people's lowest-rated competencies before we see them based on people's highest-rated competencies because the highest scores are the mirror image of the lowest scores. The higher people score in a given area, the more likely they are to score lower in an opposing area.

Most anything you do to an extreme causes problems. When you do something to an extreme, it creates an issue that either you or someone else has to offset and do to the opposite extreme to counterbalance. If you are overly assertive with an employee, you or someone else has to come back and make an apology. If you are fun-loving, someone else has to offset your free spirit with a degree of seriousness. If you are overly spontaneous, someone else has to provide a degree of organization and planning. If you are extremely optimistic, someone else has to provide the practical perspective. It is like being overly lenient with your children, and your spouse has to counterbalance your extreme leniency with constructive discipline so the kids receive balanced parenting.

As shown in Figure 1.4, there is a predictable relationship between the application of a virtue and its performance. A competence that is overused hinders performance just as much as one that is absent. Graphically, the relationship resembles an inverted U. Performance goes up with the development and application of a virtue to a point and then performance goes back down as the virtue is overused.

Figure 1.4: The Extremes of Competence

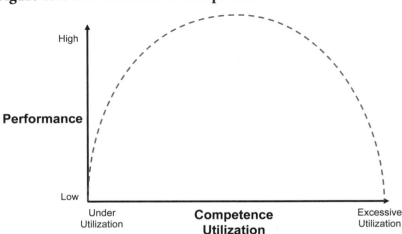

Even a highly valuable trait like the desire to learn causes issues and lowers performance when used to the extreme. It creates a tendency for people to emphasize learning over application. Even when extreme learners do apply their knowledge, they often prefer to do it on an experimental basis rather than in a productive application. They prefer knowing over doing, thus limiting the contributions they make to their organization. To the other extreme, a complete absence of a desire to learn makes people obsolete.

As another example, an absence of courage makes people slaves to their fears, where extreme courage puts people in unnecessary danger. A lack of consideration and empathy for others leads to selfishness, yet too much generosity prevents people from completing their own work and holding others accountable.

You might do something well, but it is only a strength when it is used in the proper context. Without context, a discussion about your strengths versus your weaknesses is academic. Strengths are only strengths and weaknesses are only weaknesses in specific contexts. In practice, great leaders find balance in the capabilities they employ. They develop a rich set of competencies to be applied in the appropriate situations, not merely because a competency is their "strength."

LUCK VERSUS COMPETENCE

If you keep up with contemporary leadership philosophy, you will read and hear everything imaginable. Self-proclaimed experts on leadership regularly make outlandish statements. I've heard people claim that the best leaders are people with bipolar disorder, moodiness, depression, and even psychopathy. I've heard people say that the best leaders are those who lack empathy because they can make the tough decisions. I've also heard that the best leaders are purely empathetic to the exclusion of all logic because they are completely focused on their people.

The truth is that just about any attitude or behavior in a given situation can be the best for that situation. A manager on an emotional high during the high side of bipolar disorder might very well exhibit a higher degree of energy and ability to perform for that period of time. A manager in a state of depression might also be better able to relate to an employee who is going through a crisis. However, it is more likely that the manager's depression has nothing to do with his or her ability to relate to someone's crisis and it is merely someone's incorrect opinion of correlation. Even if depression was consistently correlated with empathy, it doesn't prove causation.

A coach who yells profanities at players throughout a game might end up winning the game, but that doesn't mean the team won because of the coach's use of expletives. Even conceding that the coach's expletives made the players step up their game in one instance or for a whole game doesn't mean a cursing approach is the best for all coaches, in all sports, in all games, on all occasions. Something working once or twice doesn't make it the best solution for every situation.

People regularly miscorrelate cause and effect. Objective analyses of people's claims often find that even alleged experts make claims of correlation based on very selective circumstances. Inexperienced consultants, speakers, authors, and academics regularly make claims of correlation that have little factual basis. The typical miscorrelation in regard to leadership occurs when someone researches a highly successful company or celebrated historical figure to identify what made them so great. The researchers often start out looking for a certain characteristic and generally find what they are looking for. They then state unequivocally that because a president took a certain action, the whole company prospered. They say that because a division manager possessed a certain attribute, the division went on to achieve great performance. I occasionally read people's perspectives on IBM or other companies I've done work for on topics that I have firsthand knowledge of, and about as many get their facts wrong as those who get them right.

It is the norm for researchers to target celebrated companies and people in search of what made them successful or failures. Yet because the researchers were not a material part of the success or failure, they have to rely on other perspectives, which come with biases, rationalizations, and forgetfulness. In some cases, the researchers get it right, but often they miss important details such as a competitor's misstep or that the overall market was also growing at a record pace. As a result, misinformed researchers correlate decisions and characteristics to managers who in reality don't deserve much of the credit or blame. Nor do many researchers seem to be able to admit that luck was involved. They don't acknowledge that great results are not always the result of someone's intentional efforts. There are situations where people are simply at the right place at the right time.

There is no one competency that always correlates to any result or that perfectly fits every situation. Neither is there any dysfunctional behavior that wouldn't be a good fit for at least one situation. Only the ill-informed would say that a specific behavior *always* has to be present.

> THERE IS NO ONE COMPETENCY THAT ALWAYS CORRELATES TO ANY RESULT OR THAT PERFECTLY FITS EVERY SITUATION.

What people can accurately claim, though, is that a certain behavior or practice produces a better result more often than another. *Best practices* are not called *perfect practices* for a reason. While a practice might be the best practice in most situations, it isn't the best practice in all situations. When you follow best practices, your odds of success are high but are not 100 percent. There are many variables—especially in the context of leading and coaching people—that cause unique situations to come up in which best practices aren't always the best. Employing proven best practices is a good bet but still a bet.

While luck plays a part in isolated successes, leaders who have sustained high performance over many years—through multiple economic cycles, and through different teams of people—don't achieve it through luck. Great leaders such as coach John Wooden are consistently successful because they employ the best practices and behaviors that are most appropriate for each given situation. Sustained achievement doesn't result from the repeated use of the legendary "Hail Mary" pass that a manager might make in desperation at the end of a quarter or in a pivotal supplier negotiation. It admittedly worked for the NFL's Dallas Cowboys quarterback Roger Staubach when he completed that famous pass in desperation to Drew Pearson to beat the Minnesota Vikings in the 1975 playoffs, but it isn't an approach great leaders depend on day in and day out. An occasional desperate pass or risky decision might be just what is needed, but it isn't a sustainable strategy. Great leaders rely on behaviors that consistently give them the best odds of success. They are not one-hit wonders or lottery jackpot winners.

If you have been a beneficiary of fortuitous circumstances, congratulations. You were deserving of your good fortune because I'm sure you have also been the unfortunate recipient of unlucky circumstances. However, don't rely on luck. Luck runs out. To become a great leader over the long term, learn and apply the competencies of great leadership. Learn the competencies that put the odds of sustainable success in your favor.

Style Versus Competence

While any overused strength can be a weakness, it is important that people use their talents and unique abilities. A person with an inherent sense of humor doesn't need to become somber and stoic to become a great leader. A creative person doesn't need to become scientific. A person who loves the outdoors doesn't need to learn to do all their work in an office.

People who excel at leadership or any other domain integrate their unique abilities with the best practices of their domain. They don't supplant their innate aptitudes with sterilized domain knowledge and rigid behaviors. They instead find ways to integrate their talents with proven domain methods. They incorporate their creative interests, love of the outdoors, sense of humor, or whatever they do especially well with the proven best practices of their domain.

The SCOPE of Leadership competency model was developed with several objectives in mind. One was to leverage people's inherent abilities and accommodate their style differences. While there are many characteristics that great leaders have in common, not every characteristic is shared. What makes one person an effective leader doesn't universally make every leader effective. Some behaviors are more attributable to style differences than to competency differences. Humor, for example, is a powerful characteristic to have in many situations, but not all great leaders tell great jokes and make people cry with laughter.

Another important consideration in developing the SCOPE of Leadership framework was not to stipulate one definition of success. Success for one person is making a lot of money, where success for another is living a balanced lifestyle, protecting animals, or leaving a legacy. There is no universal definition of success. Success is in the eye of the beholder. It is dependent on a person's individual values, passions, goals, and circumstances. Being adept at leading people only dictates that there is a desired result that is achieved through the influence of people.

The competencies in the SCOPE of Leadership model apply regardless of your age, intellect, gender, style, culture, occupation, or position. They are *success-neutral* competencies that, when developed, are powerful in any context. You will apply them within your natural style and aptitudes. You will apply them personally and professionally.

What you can't do if you expect to become a great leader, however, is use your natural style and strengths as excuses for not developing a competence or using a more appropriate ability. You can't expect a desirable outcome if you inappropriately use your sense of humor in a situation that deserves respectful seriousness. You can't dismiss the importance of flexibility just because you think like a process engineer. You can't dress like a slob at a formal presentation just because you prefer to dress like a slob.

Combining your unique interests and abilities with the core competencies of great leadership requires compromises. There will be situations where you'll have to refrain from doing something that comes naturally to you in favor of using a less natural or developed ability. There will be situations where you will say nothing even though you have the answer. There will be situations where you will do nothing even though you have the ability.

The key to being a great as well as authentic leader is to be able to integrate your natural style with proven leadership competencies in a way that is most suitable for a given situation. Fortunately, it happens naturally the more you apply proven leadership competencies and become comfortable using them. You can be yourself as well as a great leader.

LEADERSHIP APPROACHES

In the industrial age of the early twentieth century, the predominant approach to leadership was *command and control*. Managers were essentially taskmasters, directing and controlling their people by telling them what to do. Management's focus was on process efficiency and asset utilization rather than people. Management's top priority was to care for and get the most out of their plants and equipment, with people taking a secondary priority. Jobs were more labor-intensive, required few advanced skills, and relegated many people to commodity status. Management's carelessness with people was also tolerated in part because employees didn't know better and there weren't many better employment options.

Contemporary leadership best practices promote a different approach. Present-day leadership philosophy is based on empowerment rather than control and coaching instead of commanding. It emphasizes obtaining the most out of people rather than processes and equipment. Systems are now designed to enable people versus people being focused on obtaining the most out of systems. The most effective leaders now encourage, guide, coach, facilitate, and enable their employees. They motivate and inspire their people rather than control or intimidate them.

This is not to say that all employees are now to be given full authority and empowerment. There are still and will always be situations that require management control and redirection. Leadership is situational; different situations deserve different approaches. Where one situation might necessitate that a leader use a calm and soothing demeanor, another might be better served with a stern demeanor. There are situations where patience is truly

> LEADERSHIP IS
> SITUATIONAL;
> DIFFERENT SITUATIONS
> DESERVE DIFFERENT
> APPROACHES.

a virtue but other situations where patience is not. If you are leading people through a crisis where there is an immediate threat of physical danger, you wouldn't start a brainstorming session and try to reach consensus. You would yell a warning and get people to start running. In contrast, you wouldn't go into a commanding and telling mode in a situation where you need a new innovative idea or to gain people's buy-in for one.

The SCOPE of Leadership model and its core competencies of great leaders don't dictate a single leadership approach. The competencies enable multiple leadership approaches that accommodate multiple situations. They enable relevant responses to most any management scenario, regardless of the nature of the work being performed or the industry you are in. They enable the multitude of roles that leaders perform, including coaching, enabling, encouraging, motivating, facilitating, aligning, organizing, prioritizing, managing, problem solving, shaping, assimilating, informing, and transforming.

These varied roles and responsibilities fall into six different leadership approaches, as depicted in Figure 1.5, that managers typically employ. Depending on the circumstances, any one of them could be the most appropriate one to use.

While it is important to a manager's effectiveness to be able to use any one of these approaches as a situation dictates, managers tend to favor one or two approaches over others. Managers who are rarely available or directly engaged with their team employ a *phantom* approach. Managers who follow the management philosophy of the industrial age most often use the *taskmaster* approach. Managers who lead small teams and use their domain skills on a regular basis use the *contributor* approach. Managers who spend most of their time prioritizing activities and allocating resources employ the *organizer* approach. Managers who focus on developing, enabling, and encouraging their people practice the *coach* approach. Managers who lead people through inspiration and organizational change use the *transformer* approach.

The last two approaches, coaching and transforming, represent the change from managing to leading. They embody leadership practices where the other approaches utilize more management oriented practices.

In my company's SCOPE of Leadership 360 assessment surveys, we assess people's tendency to use each of the six approaches in addition to assessing their core leadership competencies. The leaders who maintain the highest levels of employee engagement and consistently deliver top results utilize the *coach* approach the most. Their next most used approach is generally a tie between the *transformer* and *organizer* approaches. They use the *contributor* approach less, primarily only when they are working with more junior employees. They use the *taskmaster* approach significantly less and use the *phantom* approach only in rare circumstances. On a graph, this ideal distribution of approach utilization looks like a bell curve shifted to the right, with the top of the curve peaking on the *coach* approach as depicted by the dashed line in Figure 1.5.

Figure 1.5: Leadership Approaches

Managing ← → Leading

High ← Ideal distribution of time spent in each approach → Low

Approach	Phantom	Taskmaster	Contributor	Organizer	Coach	Transformer
Approach Description	Hands-off laissez-faire. Not present, not involved, disengaged, and often unavailable.	Leads by telling people what to do and how to do it. Enforces management policies, makes the decisions, and controls how work is performed.	Leads through the application of own domain skills and individual contribution. Focuses on execution and achieving tactical objectives.	Leads by setting goals, directing priorities, keeping people informed, bringing people together, building consensus, aligning resources, and engaging people in opportunities.	Leads by developing, facilitating, and enabling others. Helps people overcome issues. Works through others who themselves contribute, engage opportunities, and take responsibility.	Leads by motivating and inspiring others. Promotes a clear vision and strategy. Facilitates change and shapes the culture. Fosters teamwork, a spirit of unity, and innovation.
Key Focus Areas and Attributes	Absence, disconnectedness	Compliance, command, control, coercion	Tasks, tactical operations, transactions	Goals, planning, scheduling, information, resource alignment	People, skill development, facilitation, enablement, empowerment	Vision, strategy, intrinsic inspiration, organizational change, teamwork
Source of Power	Lack of availability, exclusivity	Position, control over rewards and consequences	Domain expertise, domain skills	Authority to prioritize, control over resources, relationships	Coaching skill, experience, wisdom, encouragement	Trustworthiness, communication skill, vision, ability to influence

Leaders who coach their people and transform their organizations use their leadership competence as their source of power. People follow these leaders because these leaders are competent, trustworthy, wise, and visionary. In contrast, managers who resort to a taskmaster approach rely on the authority that comes with their position. They rely on external motivators such as rewards and compensation schemes to coerce the behaviors they desire from their people. Managers who use the organizer approach rely on their relationships and roster of resources as their source of power. Contributors rely on their domain expertise and skills. Phantom managers get what they get done through the power of their limited availability or their aura of exclusivity.

Table 1.4 provides explanations for each approach with examples of situations where they are appropriate. Compare the approach you rely on most to the one that your organization needs most. If your organization needs to change in some way, yet you are employing a taskmaster approach, realize that you would be more effective at achieving change by using a transformer approach. If you are leading an organization that has more work to do than people to do it with, and you are primarily using a transformer approach, consider that you would be more effective by employing an organizer approach that emphasizes prioritization and resource optimization. Learning leadership and becoming a great leader involves developing and utilizing multiple approaches.

TABLE 1.4: LEADERSHIP APPROACHES

1. **Phantom:** Phantom leadership is a hands-off, laissez-faire approach characterized by a leader's disengagement. It is appropriate when working with seasoned, self-directed teams or when the leader has team members who have been coddled and coached but need to develop their own sense of responsibility. Phantom leaders leverage the power that comes from being absent and having limited availability.

2. **Taskmaster:** The taskmaster leadership approach is characterized by telling and directing. Its best application is in working with low-skilled labor or situations that need to be carefully controlled, such as those involving human safety. It is also appropriate in a crisis mode where people need to do exactly what they are told and do it in a hurry. It is appropriate when policies need to be followed or there are strict compliance standards that need to be adhered to. Taskmasters influence people through their power of position and control over rewards and bonuses.

3. **Contributor:** Contributor leadership is performing hands-on individual contributor work, albeit at a senior level. It is appropriate when leaders are working with team members to transfer skills, need to demonstrate their commitment, or are in situations that require their advanced expertise. It is also appropriate when managers lead small teams and their job is as much to contribute as it is to lead. Managers' focus when acting as contributors is primarily on completing tasks and transactions rather than on people and skill development. They focus on tactical operational execution with themselves being a key part of the organization's execution capability. Contributors influence others through the power that comes from being skilled domain experts.

4. **Organizer:** The organizer approach to leadership is characterized by a focus on aligning and allocating resources. It is particularly applicable in large organizations or matrix structures where the equivalent of a traffic cop is needed. It is also appropriate for situations where demand outstrips supply and someone is needed to prioritize projects and the assignment of resources to those projects. The organizer manager often works in an environment where people are assigned to projects from specialist pools of resources. Organizers spend much of their time planning, adjusting priorities, allocating resources, and disseminating information. They influence people through the power that comes with having relationships, information, and control over resources.

5. **Coach:** A coaching approach to leadership is characterized by a focus on employee development and empowerment. It is a focus on people rather than tasks. Coaching as a management approach moves from a managerial orientation to a leader orientation. Coaching emphasizes developing people's skills so that individuals can contribute and organize on their own initiative. Coaches spend their time helping people develop and overcoming issues that prevent people from improving their performance. Coaches influence people through the power that comes with their coaching skills, wisdom, insight, and encouragement.

6. **Transformer:** Transformer leadership is characterized by effecting change. It is about crafting a vision and inspiring people to follow it. This is the approach great leaders employ when changing an organization's direction as markets shift. It involves leading people through organizational change. It is motivating people to work together as a team, give their best effort, and strive for the highest levels of performance. While not an approach that is needed all the time, it is the pinnacle of great leadership. Transformers influence people through the power that comes from their vision, charisma, ability to influence people, and overall leadership competence.

"And" Thinking

As authors Jim Collins and Jerry Porras emphasized in their best-selling book *Built to Last*, success is not based on performing one activity versus another. It is achieved through multiple activities. It is based on the genius of the *and* rather than the tyranny of the *or*. Sustained growth, for example, is achieved through delivering short-term results while also delivering long-term results. Top sales performance is based on delivering products at an attractive price as well as at a high level of quality. Market-share gains come through bold moves that also employ risk-mitigation measures.

This same *and* philosophy applies to leadership. Leadership isn't about promoting a vision versus operating with excellence. It isn't about strategy versus execution or about processes or systems versus people. Leadership is not about any single competence or focus. You can have a great vision, but it is meaningless without great people to execute it. You might have a phenomenal capacity to execute with excellence, but if you are executing against a bad strategy or producing a product the market doesn't want, it is meaningless.

Great leaders are not one-dimensional. Rather than have a singular focus, they use *and* thinking. They are able to balance competing issues and priorities. They blend traditional dichotomies. They effectively deal with shades of gray rather than black-and-white absolutes. When a situation requires it, rather than think in terms of all or nothing, they consider a third option. They find the optimal place in between. They deliberate, blend, and balance multiple considerations.

Leadership is about finding the delicate balance between areas that others might say can't coexist. Leaders accept themselves and desire to improve. They pursue meaning and money. They enjoy the journey and pursue a definitive destination. They encourage their employees and hold them accountable. Table 1.5 provides a list of some of the typical dichotomies that great leaders balance and blend.

TABLE 1.5: DICHOTOMIES THAT LEADERS BALANCE

• Low cost and high quality	• Praise and admonishment
• Boldness and risk mitigation	• Humility and confidence
• Flexibility and consistency	• Meaning and money
• Innovation and structure	• Journey and destination
• Strategy and execution	• Attitude and behavior
• Vision and details	• Effort and results
• Processes and people	• Acceptance and improvement
• Controls and empowerment	• Local and remote
• Instinct and data	• Doing and enabling
• Telling and listening	• Coaching and teaching

- Teams and individuals
- Staff and field
- Stability and adaptability
- Urgency and patience
- Open-mindedness and decisiveness
- Short-term and long-term

- Stockholders and employees
- Customers and partners
- Leading and following
- Candor and politeness
- Encouragement and accountability

Managers who don't realize what it takes to be a great leader are not as concerned with these dichotomies. They often oversimplify leadership and try to make it one-dimensional. They say that leadership is simply focusing on one or a few areas. The reality is that the highest levels of results are achieved by employing multiple approaches and integrating multiple competencies. Leadership isn't following a few simple ideals.

It would be wonderful if knowing how to become a great leader only required reading a simple fable in a short book, but it doesn't happen that way. Any great leader, coach, or leadership expert knows that leadership is too multidimensional to be condensed into a few simple principles. As coach John Wooden knew, the enablement of peak performance requires getting into details. It requires being able to change people's attitudes, build new behaviors, and assimilate people into teams. If being a great leader were as simple as something like focusing on the results, all people would need is the ability to read reports.

In my training programs and coaching, I strive to make learning as straightforward as possible, but there is a point at which simplification goes too far and people don't learn what they need to learn to effectively put it into practice. It is unfortunately too common that trainers as well as managers, authors, and speakers make the mistake of glossing over the real issues that need to be confronted. Great leadership requires understanding details, getting to know people's struggles, and using a broad variety of competencies to deal with them. Oversimplification is a primary reason that great leadership remains elusive for many organizations. Learning how to become a great leader isn't as simple as doing three or four things or reading a short book.

Managers compound the problem by having an oversimplified view of their role. Some are successful in the role of a manager, but when they need to coach people, lead a team in a new direction, or transform their organization in some way, their oversimplified management philosophy breaks down. The management philosophy that performance comes by simply hiring good people, holding them accountable to key measurements, and letting them do their job is flawed. It misses the reality that achieving the highest levels of performance also requires enabling, encouraging, coaching, and assimilating.

> THE MANAGEMENT PHILOSOPHY THAT PERFORMANCE COMES BY SIMPLY HIRING GOOD PEOPLE, HOLDING THEM ACCOUNTABLE TO KEY MEASUREMENTS, AND LETTING THEM DO THEIR JOB IS FLAWED.

It should be no surprise that leadership requires multiple competencies. A good craftsman requires many tools. Surgeons use hundreds of procedures. Doctors have thousands of medical remedies and medicines at their disposal. Engineers learn and pick from hundreds of formulas. Writers have to know and use tens of thousands of words. It shouldn't be difficult to expect that leaders need to employ a multitude of competencies and approaches.

Fortunately, once you become a great leader, leadership becomes simpler. As with any learned behavior, leading becomes easier as it becomes habit. It also looks simpler to others because people don't generally see a great leader's entire tool belt of leadership tools at one time. People see only the few tools being used in a given situation.

BECOMING COMPETENT

Learning leadership competence isn't any more impossible than learning a foreign language, a new sport, or most any skill. There are many people in the world who know multiple languages. There are project managers who manage multiple projects and salespeople who handle multiple accounts. There are coaches who coach many executives and consultants who advise many companies. The human mind is far more capable than most people know and take advantage of.

Leadership competencies, secondary languages, athletic skills, or other domains that are applied repeatedly become embedded into your subconscious. Over time and with application, knowledge and behaviors become as embedded in you as your genes are. With application, you move your knowledge and ability into your vast unconscious mental reserves. Once a competence is engrained, you don't have to think consciously to use it. It is always in the background, ready to come to your service when a situation arises where you need it, but doesn't take up conscious resources when you don't. Your mind is free to take in more knowledge and learn other competencies. Your immense subconscious mental ability and long-term memory enable you to reach seemingly impossible levels of knowledge and competence if you take advantage of them.

To make learning leadership straightforward, focus on one competency at a time. Fully immerse yourself into developing one area. Apply what you learn to the point that it becomes natural to you and moves into your subconscious. Then turn your attention to the next competency. Continually repeat the process, and over time you will learn the competencies required to become a great leader.

The remaining five books of the SCOPE of Leadership series are provided for this purpose. They make learning leadership as straightforward as possible. Each chapter covers one of thirty-eight core competencies of great leaders. The books are designed to be read one chapter at a time, providing you with the detailed information you need to put the chapter's competency into application. The chapters are not long, but each one provides a substantial amount of content, examples, and information for future reference. The chapters you will read that cover areas in which you are already adept will be quick and easy readings. As you read chapters on areas that you need to work on, slow down and let the material sink in. I suggest you take notes, reflect on them, discuss them with others, and put them into practice before moving on to the next chapter.

If you are part of a group of aspiring leaders or involved in a leadership training program, leverage the SCOPE of Leadership book series as a team learning resource. Create a team-based book club. Book clubs that study nonfiction books provide a great opportunity for informal learning. They provide an easy and economical method for people to stay current on contemporary thought leadership. Combined with the collective wisdom, engagement, and accountability that small groups provide, team book clubs provide valuable augmentation to formal training programs. They leverage both the convenience of self-directed learning, as people are able to read on their own schedule, and the power that comes from working together as a group.

Book clubs also create important dialogue in organizations that managers and human resource professionals sometimes have difficulty creating. In particular, book clubs stimulate three important conversations: ones that employees want to have with their bosses, those that bosses want to have with their employees, and conversations employees want to have with their peers. Book content—by virtue of being third-party material—provides a conduit for discussing difficult topics in a way that can be more appropriate than directly confronting someone's actual behaviors. People often have a boss, employee, or peer with whom they would like to have a delicate dialogue, yet neither formal meetings nor hallway chats are conducive to their topic. An informal book club, however, provides the opportunity. It enables dialogue on sensitive topics without targeting individuals. It enables you to challenge people as a group to put a given competence into practice without targeting a single individual. Of course, where the setting is appropriate to target a single individual, the book content enables that as well.

Make learning leadership fun and engaging. Do it as part of a formal book club or informal small group. Invite your colleagues, family, or friends to join you. There is no better or more economical way to get the most out of your reading.

For your reference, Table 1.6 lists ten steps to running an effective team book club.

TABLE 1.6: STEPS TO RUNNING AN EFFECTIVE TEAM BOOK CLUB

1. Recruit one to two others to join you in sponsoring a book club in your organization. Bosses are great to include because you want to ensure the club has their approval and support.

2. Craft simple guidelines by which you will conduct your book club. Include the types of books you expect to read, meeting frequency, meeting venue, duration, and expectations of involvement.

3. Ensure the book club guidelines facilitate the goals and benefits you are looking for in your club and organization. Emphasize the importance of goals, such as individual learning, stimulating dialogue, improving team performance, developing best practices, and staying current on contemporary thought leadership.

4. Aim for a group size of five to ten people to enable everyone to be engaged in the discussions. If your group has more than ten people, break it up and start multiple clubs. When you have your group members set, review and finalize the club guidelines with everyone.

5. Pick your first book to read and have everyone obtain a copy (or coordinate the purchase through one person). Agree on the number of chapters you will read in each reading period. Keep it within one chapter or about one hundred pages per reading interval so you don't exceed people's time constraints.

6. Disseminate book club discussion questions that you plan to discuss prior to your scheduled chapter review meetings. They might be specific to the chapter being read or general ones you will use at every meeting. The questions should facilitate dialog on the main themes of the chapter, how the themes apply to people, and how the underlying principles will be put into productive use.

7. Ensure everyone in the discussion contributes and has a chance to offer comments. Close the chapter review meetings by having each person give a brief summary of what they found most meaningful in the chapter and how they plan to apply it in the coming week.

8. Confirm the reading assignment for the next book section and the time of the next meeting before adjourning the meeting.

9. Repeat the reading assignments and team discussions until the book is finished. At about two to three weeks prior to the conclusion of each book, confirm the next book to be read.

10. To maintain book club member engagement, rotate responsibility between each person for choosing the books to read. Rotate, too, the discussion group leader responsibility for each discussion group meeting. Share the responsibility of supplying snacks or collecting the food orders if meeting during a meal. If you have the budget, buy lunch for the team when they meet. Providing food is a great way to ensure people show up and one of the least expensive training programs you will ever pay for!

In addition to team book clubs, other popular approaches to learning leadership include team coaching, one-on-one coaching, training programs, off-site boot camps, special projects, and customized long-term development programs. These programs are significantly more expensive and time-consuming but have the advantage of professional facilitation and training that don't come with team book clubs or individual reading. Take advantage of all of them if you can.

When I help organizations create leadership development curriculums, we include multiple learning approaches. In a typical one-year leadership development program, we include quarterly if not monthly training seminars. We include assessments such as 360 surveys and personality assessments. We include special assignments that involve completing projects, shadowing people, and reading books. We include monthly or bi-monthly coaching sessions. We also include tests and certifications where appropriate. It is an intense year for the participants, but at the end of the program they are ready and able to take on most any leadership situation that comes their way.

Whatever your learning need, budget, or situation, get started and do something. Select the learning approach that is most appropriate for you and your team. You as well as your organization, community, and family will benefit significantly from it. The chances are good that the people around you who could benefit the most from learning are the least likely to request it. Make it a priority to involve them with you.

PRINCIPLES IN REVIEW

Here are key principles from this chapter to keep in mind.

- **Development:** People become great leaders through behaviors, conscious thought, unconscious thought, and circumstances, all of which you have influence if not direct control over.
- **Strengths:** Utilize your strengths, but don't overuse them. Overused or misused strengths become weaknesses.
- **Luck:** Leverage luck whenever you can, but don't depend on it. Luck isn't a sustainable strategy.

- **Leadership Tools:** Leadership is situational. Employ the right leadership tool, style, and approach for the situation. It is no more appropriate to always be a coach than it is to always be an organizer, taskmaster, or transformer.
- **"And" Thinking:** Do both of something when you need to do both. It's not sufficient to do one versus another when both are needed.
- **Capacity to Learn:** The human brain has an incredible capacity to learn, know, and do. Use it.
- **Learning:** Learning occurs in many ways, including formal and informal methods. Find the method, or mix of methods, that work for you and put them into practice.

CHAPTER FOUR

DISRUPTIVE TRENDS
AFFECTING LEADERSHIP

The art of progress is to preserve order amid change and to preserve change amid order.

—Alfred North Whitehead

As the saying goes, the only constant in this world is change. The twenty-first century has been no exception. Change has not just continued; in many ways it has accelerated. The pace of technological innovation and globalization has been especially astonishing. The seemingly overnight widespread adoption of online social media, for example, not only created new billionaires but also connected and reconnected people in ways that were never before possible. Family members who live thousands of miles apart can know as much about each other's activities as they would if they lived in the same neighborhood. Old friends who had lost touch can know what the other is doing every day.

The ubiquitous access to information, communications, and advanced Internet applications has enabled levels of productivity and knowledge unlike anything the world has ever experienced.

Employees, customers, and competitors have access to information that before was difficult if not impossible to obtain. Products and services are widely adopted or disparaged with the push of a button. Countries and political regimes are being overthrown because of citizens' new awareness of their leaders' depravity and people's ability to assemble support for new authorities.

Geographical boundaries have become unimportant in many industries. Ideas are now shared globally as easily as locally. Products and services are provided by companies all over the world with little consideration about their country of origin. Never before has global commerce been so easy and widespread. Even small businesses in small countries that never before operated outside of their local geographical boundaries are now engaging in global commerce. Political, social, and economic changes are rampant due to recent technological advancements.

There is also a dark side to the ubiquity of communications and globalization. Evil and shame have new channels of communications and access. Terrorism and corruption no longer have geographical boundaries. Workplaces, schools, cities, and countries have to worry about security in ways never needed before. With most information and identities now being controlled electronically, information security has become of extreme importance. The more virtual the world becomes, the more information security becomes equivalent to physical security.

THE MORE VIRTUAL THE WORLD BECOMES, THE MORE INFORMATION SECURITY BECOMES EQUIVALENT TO PHYSICAL SECURITY.

The world is changing in unprecedented ways. Even areas of life and work that have traditionally been relatively stable are undergoing change. The very concept of stability itself is undergoing change as it shifts from a desirable quality to an undesirable one. Any technology, skill, process, system, or product that has been around for more than a few years is assumed to be old and obsolete. Change is the new normal. How customers buy, organizations operate, employees think, and hence leaders lead are no exceptions.

Many of the principles of great leadership have been around for thousands of years and will never change. Because people are people, many aspects of dealing with people are timeless. People have always needed and will always need to share ideas, have relationships, and be part of groups. People will always have a need to be encouraged and appreciated. They will always enjoy the comfort, convenience, and rewards of achievement. However, what people do and how they do it has changed, and that can't be ignored.

There are many recent developments that leaders need to be aware of and take into consideration. Table 1.7 lists five of the more significant changes that are especially disruptive to how leaders lead.

TABLE 1.7: TRENDS DISRUPTING THE LEADERSHIP STATUS QUO		
Historical Normal		**New Normal**
Money	→	Meaning
Ignorance	→	Information
Commanding	→	Coaching
Independence	→	Interdependence
Burnout	→	Balance

As a result of these shifts away from historical norms, managers are encountering resistance to old approaches to management. Managers are discovering that the sources of power they utilized in the past, such as their position, control over people's compensation, and access to information, are no longer reliable sources of power. Managers are learning that ideas and methods that were effective in the past are now ineffective. They are finding old practices to be unconvincing, slow, and unaffordable. What some managers considered normal management practices earlier in their careers are now obsolete. Managers who expect to stay relevant and effective have to utilize new practices, leverage new sources of power, and learn new ways to lead.

The SCOPE of Leadership framework incorporates both timeless principles of leadership and contemporary leadership best practices. It takes into consideration what is now possible through technological advancements and global commerce. It accommodates the new realities of the twenty-first century. The remainder of this chapter provides a brief explanation of the five trending developments that are having a dramatic impact on the way workers think and how contemporary leaders are responding.

MONEY IS BEING SUPPLANTED BY MEANING

Historically, people have worked for money. A job was viewed as an activity that was pursued primarily as a source of income. Working was what people did to earn the money they needed in order to do what they really wanted to do. Working was the means to an end.

While money is still important, it is no longer the primary factor many people look for in a job. Employee surveys find that once people make enough money to satisfy their basic needs, they place more value on other characteristics of their work. Employees want to enjoy their work. They want to perform work that is gratifying and satisfying. They want to work with people they enjoy being around and in a culture they enjoy being part of. They want to perform work that is meaningful and aligned to their values.

For people who have reached a level of income that affords an adequate lifestyle, meaning has replaced money as the primary attribute they look for when looking for employment. People expect to work for organizations and in environments that satisfy their emotional, intellectual, social, and philosophical needs as much as their financial needs. People now view their work as much an end as they do a means to an end.

People no longer have much interest or tolerance for making money for the sake of making money. They are disgusted with the corporate and political greed they witnessed earlier in their lives. They are opposed to increasing profits at the expense of

> PEOPLE NOW VIEW THEIR WORK AS MUCH AN END AS THEY DO A MEANS TO AN END.

the environment. They are more concerned about causing irreversible climate changes than reaching a record profit. People don't tolerate the exploitation of other people, animals, the climate, or nature merely to provide investors with a better financial return on their investment.

Leaders are finding that to attract top talent they have to provide jobs that are satisfying and meaningful. They can't simply offer people high-paying salaries and stock options. They can't use financial incentives to make up for unattractive jobs in unattractive industries or for having to work for unlikable managers.

Leaders are finding they have to provide a vision that is compelling for their employees as much as they do for their customers and stockholders. They have to provide an appealing workplace culture with values that align with their employees' values. They have to demonstrate good stewardship of their resources. They have to be respectful of their communities and the environment. They have to demonstrate corporate social responsibility.

When considering where to work, many people place as much importance on what a company does to make the world a better place as they do on benefits, salaries, and the organization's viability. Employees want to be part of something consequential. They want their workplace to be a source of pride and satisfaction. They want their workplace to reinforce their personal values and core identity.

Top performers have many choices in where to work. To compete for top talent, organizations can no longer simply rely on polished recruiting campaigns, big salaries, company equity, or fat bonuses. Managers can no longer use money as their crutch to make up for their controlling nature, uninteresting jobs, uncompelling vision, unethical values, or dearth of corporate responsibility. People place more importance on working in environments that are aligned to their moral values and interests. People want to enjoy their work.

Ignorance Is Being Eliminated by Information

With the ubiquity of wireless communications and Internet access, most everyone is only a click away from instant access to information. If someone wants to know something, they can know it within a few seconds. All they need to do is make a query on their device. Information is no longer difficult to obtain. It is no longer for the chosen few. It is no longer a source of power. It is accessible to everyone.

Everyone is in constant contact. What took months to communicate prior to the nineteenth century and took hours to know in the twentieth century has turned into seconds in the twenty-first century. Everyone has instant access to everyone and everything. Data, facts, locations, audio, video, and pictures on most any topic are now available simply by asking.

Much of what was hidden or confidential in the past is now public. What was unclear is now transparent. No longer can organizations hide their inequities and wrongdoings. No longer are the complaints of unsatisfied employees, suppliers, or customers kept secret. No longer can leaders expect their words and actions to be kept private. Executives, managers, preachers, teachers, community leaders, and politicians know immediately whether what they did or said is popular or unpopular. Within seconds, anyone can discover what other people are thinking, doing, buying, studying, playing, performing, liking, or disliking.

No longer is having information a source of differentiation. Information is a commodity. Everyone has it. Intermediaries that relied on having privileged information have gone out of business. Managers who had power because of what they knew have lost their power. Forecasts, strategies, methods, models, recipes, ingredients, profit margins, and compensations are in the public domain. People can no longer make a living based on owning information. For information to be valuable, people have to do something with it that adds value. They have to interpret information and convert it into something more valuable. Differentiation is now based on how information is applied—on putting information into productive use rather than on simply having it.

Like it or not, transparency is the new normal. Information has replaced ignorance and isolation. Most anything you do that can be observed by others, directly or indirectly, will find its way into the public domain. What you say, write, or do that is observed or caught on camera will become public knowledge. Leaders have to be extremely careful about what they and their organizations say and do. They have to concern themselves with how the general public will interpret anything and everything. The new normal is being informed rather than being ignorant. The only people who are ignorant about what is going on in the world are those who choose to be ignorant. Information is no longer limited to the privileged few.

COMMANDING IS BEING EXCHANGED FOR COACHING

Managers who in the past used a commanding, controlling, telling, or intimidating approach to management are finding that it is no longer effective. Like soldiers who realize they are out of ammunition, command-and-control-style managers are finding they are no longer powerful and influential. Simply because managers are in management and have the authority to hire, fire, promote, and determine pay raises no longer guarantees that employees will respect them. People have too many choices of where to work and too little patience to put up with being controlled like a puppet or treated like a piece of equipment. People expect respect.

> LIKE SOLDIERS WHO REALIZE THEY ARE OUT OF AMMUNITION, COMMAND-AND-CONTROL-STYLE MANAGERS ARE FINDING THEY ARE NO LONGER POWERFUL AND INFLUENTIAL.

People want to use their brain in their work. They want to make an important contribution. They expect to be empowered and work with a degree of independence. They want to have their own authority and responsibility. They want to have a say in the organization they work for and the work they perform. People are no longer willing simply to follow procedures and do as they are told.

People know they are an organization's most important and strategic asset. They know the organization's level of quality, service, responsiveness, differentiation, and profitability is in their hands. People are no longer simply putting part *A* into hole *B* on an assembly line as their parents or grandparents might have done; they play a much more valuable role and expect to be treated accordingly.

The days when managers barked orders to their employees, rebuked them in public, or threatened them are largely over. Not only is intimidation ineffective, it is considered bullying and harassment—either of which is grounds for termination and the basis for legal action. For managers to lead people effectively now, they have to inspire and motivate. They must be polite and empathetic. They must be caring and considerate. They must use their brain rather than their brawn. Managers can't merely rely on the power of their position or level of their authority. They have to earn people's respect based on the person they are, the leadership qualities they possess, and the leadership behaviors they exemplify.

As with managers who historically relied on the power of intimidation or private information, managers who have historically relied on spreadsheets and measurements to do their management work for them are finding themselves without a job. Employees expect to be treated as individuals, not numbers. Employees expect recognition for not only results but also effort. They expect individualized attention. They expect help and encouragement, not just monitoring and tracking. They expect coaching and great leadership.

The annual performance appraisal process is also changing and in some cases being eliminated. The once-annual event that provided managers and employees with an opportunity to talk about performance and improvement is being replaced with ongoing coaching. No longer is it acceptable for managers to meet with their employees once a year to talk about improvement opportunities. Yearly performance discussions have been replaced with monthly or even weekly coaching conversations. Performance evaluations are turning into development plans that are continuously reviewed and updated.

In addition to helping people improve, leaders as coaches are spending more time encouraging their employees. Leadership is not only developing employees and holding them accountable but also ensuring they have the optimal mindset to do their job. Effective managers are spending more time in a cheerleading role. They are giving their employees regular pep talks and praise. Where managers might have only provided praise and encouragement on an infrequent basis before, they now find the need to give it on a weekly if not daily basis.

Effective managers are also giving more attention to enabling their employees. Managers are ensuring their employees have the resources and tools they need in order to do their job. No longer are managers primarily focused on obtaining the most productivity out of their plants and equipment but rather on obtaining the most out of their employees. Managers are more focused than ever on leveraging technology and how machines, tools, and systems can help boost the productivity of their employees. Managers are now concentrating on enabling employee productivity and performance rather than dictating it.

Independence Is Shifting to Interdependence

Many organizations in the past were vertically integrated and produced most of their own products and services. That is no longer the case. It is no longer affordable for organizations to produce and provide most everything on their own. To be competitive, organizations must leverage the scale, presence, capability, and lower-cost alternatives provided by other organizations. Organizational *independence* is being replaced by organizational *interdependence*.

The level of performance and sophistication required to be competitive in the marketplace has all but eliminated those who perform at a mediocre level. No longer can an organization do something in-house at an average level of quality or cost. If they can't do it competitively, they have to let someone else do it. They have to partner with a best-in-class provider or they run the risk of going out of business.

When organizations are no longer able to perform a task at a competitive level, they turn to outsiders who can. When an organization lacks scale, geographic presence, fulfillment, distribution, or relationships, they turn to outsiders who have it. When they have limited experience, capabilities, offerings, or capacity, they more often build partnerships rather than buy or build it themselves.

Communications technology and globalization have removed physical barriers to trade and allowed ventures and partnerships to form that were not possible before. Now there are new sources of inexpensive labor, materials, and capabilities. Even if you operate a small business that provides a product or services only on a domestic basis, you can't ignore globalization. You can't ignore the low costs of goods and services provided by global suppliers. You can't ignore the new competitors coming in from global markets. Your geographic boundary is no longer going to keep you safe and secure. To remain competitive, you have to think globally. You have to leverage others' capabilities. You have to leverage partnerships. You have to be competitive in every dimension.

Managers can no longer be internally focused. They need to work effectively not only with their employees and other teams in their own organization but also with teams in other organizations. Managers need to know how to collaborate as much as they know how to compete. They need to know how to make internal versus external sourcing decisions. They need to know how to negotiate and manage contracts. They need to be able to influence and lead people whom they have no direct control over. They need to cultivate and maintain external relationships continuously. They must move from independence to interdependence.

> MANAGERS NEED TO KNOW HOW TO COLLABORATE AS MUCH AS THEY KNOW HOW TO COMPETE.

The trend of leveraging others is no surprise. It has been an important management practice for years, just not as easy to implement as it is now. Now managers are making others outside of their organization as much a part of their organization as they do their own team members. Matrix management structures, cross-departmental teams, and interorganizational partnerships are now the norm more than the exception. In many organizations, you don't even know if the people you are working with, the products you are using, or the services you are taking advantage of are from your organization or someone else's.

BURNOUT IS BEING TRADED FOR BALANCE

Employees are increasingly less interested in being slaves to their jobs. They are tired of long working hours, working on weekends, and giving up their personal life. They don't want to live merely to work. They want meaningful work, but they don't want to die of a stress-related stroke. They don't want to give up their family life and friendships as they watched their parents do. They don't want to give up their daily exercise for early morning meetings with high-fat doughnuts. They don't want to burn out. They want balance between their work life and their personal life.

People will work hard, but they won't give up their health, family, and friendships for the sake of helping their organization make its quarterly profit target. Where past generations might have put their work ahead of everything else, new generations are less inclined to do so. New generations want balance and flexibility.

One of the most important benefits prospective employees look for when considering a new job is flexible working hours and locations. People want to be able to take their children to school, have lunch with their spouse, and participate in their family's activities. They want to spend time with friends, participate in sports, and pursue hobbies. They want to work late some evenings in exchange for being able to come in a little late the next morning. They want to work longer hours Monday through Thursday so they can take off on Friday afternoon and enjoy a long weekend with their friends or family.

People want to work from home. They don't want to spend two or more hours a day fighting traffic to get to and from their office. They don't want to drop off their children at daycare before the sun comes up and pick them up after dark. They don't want to waste their time putting on makeup and dressing up only to sit at a desk and talk on the phone all day. If they have to work long hours, they want to be able to do so from the comfort of their home office, if not their boat, the beach, or their vacation condo.

Managers who expect to keep their top talent need to provide their employees with reasonable flexibility in working environments and schedules. Managers need to work out accommodations and compromises that achieve the goals of the organization while also addressing the personal needs of their employees. No longer can managers simply say "take it or leave it." More often than not their employees will leave it.

Effective managers are more aware of their employees' stress and potential for burnout than managers of the past. Managers now know they can't simply keep piling the work on their employees without giving them a break. Managers now give more attention to their employees' working conditions. They ensure their employees have some downtime. They monitor their employees' health and stress. They provide in-house fitness training or memberships to fitness centers. They provide healthy food choices in their cafeterias and healthy snacks in their vending machines. Rather than churn and burn their employees, they care for them and nurture them.

People are still people, but what people desire and do has changed. The principles by which trade is conducted have changed. The way in which work is performed has changed. So, too, has leadership. Great leaders are adapting to the new normal. They are learning how to leverage technology, globalization, and partnerships. They are learning the competencies required to be effective in working with the new generation of workers. They are learning to be great coaches, encouragers, enablers, assimilators, and managers.

PRINCIPLES IN REVIEW

Here are key principles from this chapter to keep in mind.

- **Meaning:** Provide jobs to people that connect with their values and give them a sense of professional and personal fulfillment.
- **Information:** Expect everything you do or say to be in the public domain. Expect others to be informed about everything imaginable.

- **Coaching:** Coach, enable, and encourage others rather than command, control, or intimidate them.
- **Interdependence:** Leverage the skills, relationships, capacity, scale, and costs of others both inside and outside of your organization. Don't be impeded by organizational or geographical boundaries.
- **Balance:** Provide people with accommodation for their personal needs to the extent fulfillment of their needs can satisfactorily coexist with the organization's needs.

CHAPTER FIVE

LEADERSHIP COMPETENCIES

Great leadership consists of possessing several 'building blocks' of capabilities, each complementing the others.
— Jack Zenger and Joseph Folkman

Regardless of the sport, there are five capabilities that determine an athlete's performance. Winning and losing essentially come down to these five qualities. They are listed in Table 1.8. The first letter of each attribute spells out the acronym TEMPT. Think of these as the attributes that *tempt* people to perform their best.

TABLE 1.8: FIVE CAPABILITIES THAT DETERMINE ATHLETIC PERFORMANCE
T—Technique
E—Equipment
M—Mental fitness
P—Physical fitness
T—Teamwork

Whether an athlete is competing in soccer, golf, baseball, skiing, motorsports, or any other sport, these five qualities differentiate the losers from the winners. If you don't use the correct technique, have the proper frame of mind, have the physical strength or endurance, employ the right equipment, and leverage the help of others, you don't win.

These same five qualities enable top performers at work. From a technique perspective, top performers are skilled and technically competent. They have the ability to perform their role expertly and fulfill their responsibilities. From an equipment perspective, top performers have the enabling tools and equipment required for their position. They have the facilities, supplies, systems, templates, devices, and other resources needed to perform their role.

From a mental fitness perspective, top performers are positive and mentally acute. They have a can-do attitude. They are passionate about their work and driven to achieve their goals. From a physical fitness perspective, top performers are energetic and able to handle the physical demands of their job. Their strength, endurance, effort, and positive physical self-image reinforce their confidence. Their physical fitness enhances their mental acuity and mental fitness.

From a teamwork perspective, top performers leverage the support and help of others around them. They receive assistance from others. They leverage others' capabilities, particularly in areas in which they are not as proficient. They leverage others' resources. They benefit from others' experience, advice, encouragement, facilitation, and coaching.

Great coaches and managers alike emphasize these five qualities. They help their people develop their skills and leverage their abilities. They equip their people with resources, information, systems, tools, and processes that enable high productivity and quality of execution. They encourage and exhort their people to believe in themselves and develop a can-do attitude. They have their people practice, build strength, apply effort, and cultivate endurance. They foster collaboration and teamwork.

People's capabilities in these five areas determine their level of performance in most any field, role, or pursuit. Because results don't come by focusing on results, great coaches and leaders alike target the underlying behaviors and attitudes that enable these five qualities. The competencies used by great leaders—and therefore, those in the SCOPE of Leadership framework—emphasize the development of these five qualities.

As this chapter now starts to describe the SCOPE of Leadership framework and the principles behind it, you will see that the framework emphasizes not only the techniques required to build a given competency but also the required mental fitness, physical fitness, enabling resources, and support from others.

HIERARCHY AND DEPENDENCY

There is a hierarchy in leadership development that most people don't understand. Leadership competencies don't stand in isolation. They don't merely happen randomly, or in alphabetical order. Leadership competencies have dependencies on other leadership competencies. There are foundational competencies that support higher-level competencies that support other higher-level competencies. As well, higher-level competencies reinforce lower-level

> THERE IS A HIERARCHY IN LEADERSHIP DEVELOPMENT THAT MOST PEOPLE DON'T UNDERSTAND.

competencies. The competency of *motivating others,* competency 18 in book 3, for example, depends on the subcompetency of *conveying a positive attitude,* competency 12 in book 3, and is also reinforced by the supercompetency of *knowing individuals,* competency 20 in book 4. In other words, the more you know a person, the better you are able to motivate them—and being a great motivator depends on having a positive attitude. The competency of conveying a positive attitude in turn depends on the enabling attribute of *having an attitude of gratitude* and is reinforced by the higher-level enabling attribute of *having compassion for others*. In other words, the more compassion you have for others, the more understanding and positive you will be, the more motivating you will be, and the more likely you are truly to get to know others.

The hierarchy of leadership is akin to Maslow's hierarchy of human needs depicted in Figure 1.6. You wouldn't expect someone to seek recognition or fulfillment of a personal purpose if they weren't first able to satisfy their basic physiological needs of food, water, shelter, and air. It wouldn't make sense to have a conversation about seeking self-actualization with a starving person in a Third World country. The higher-level qualities in Maslow's hierarchy also reinforce the lower-level ones. A higher-level quality like self-esteem, for example, reinforces your reputation and sense of belonging.

Figure 1.6: Hierarchy of Needs

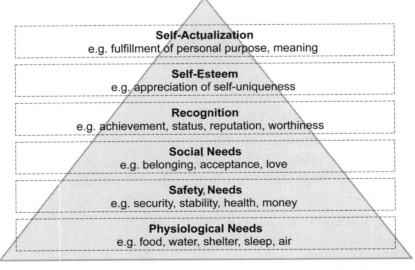

Adapted from the five levels in Abraham Maslow's original "Hierarchy of Needs"

Similarly in leadership development, it doesn't make sense to try to build a higher-order leadership competency if you haven't yet developed its foundational competencies. That is the reason reliable leadership development isn't accomplished by pursuing a random list of competencies. It requires understanding the interdependencies of competencies and developing competence in the foundational levels before attempting to build the higher-order competencies.

At the foundation of great leadership, as with great athletic performance, are the basics. The basics include rudimentary principles such as setting goals, exercising self-control, and developing courage. As you move up the SCOPE of Leadership hierarchy into more advanced leadership competencies, being competent in the basics is critical. If you don't perform the basics well, your performance in the more advanced competencies will be limited. Small issues in the fundamental competencies become amplified in the more advanced ones. The competencies of *stimulating engagement,* competency 29 in book 5, and *enabling speed and quality*, competency 34 in book 6, for example, are only made possible by performing basics such as *believing with passion,* competency 1 in book 2, and *working productively,* competency 9 in book 2.

As another example, improving teamwork and gaining the synergies that come with collaboration are critical capabilities for leaders. To do so, though, requires multiple subcompetencies. Therefore, the SCOPE of Leadership framework provides the enabling attributes to improving teamwork in *collaborating*, competency 31 in book 5. These attributes build on the attributes found in the prior chapter on *managing conflict*, competency 30, which are critical because people don't always get along. The attributes required to manage conflict build on the attributes in preceding chapters on *building community* and *creating alignment*— competencies 28 and 27. The higher the level of the competency you seek to build, the more dependencies it has on lower-level competencies.

Because the higher-level competencies and their enabling attributes also reinforce the lower-level ones, leadership competencies are recursive. They synergistically strengthen each other. For example, improving people's mental and physical energy stimulates their level of engagement. Engaged employees inspire others to become more engaged. Being a part of an inspired team in turn creates more energy. The same attributes work in reverse. Inspired people become more engaged. Engaged people are more energetic. The more energy people have, the more inspiring they are. If this sounds confusing, don't worry about it. The SCOPE of Leadership competency model takes into consideration these interdependencies so you don't have to.

The SCOPE of Leadership is like a problem map, which is discussed in more detail in the section on problem solving in the chapter on *enabling performance*, competency 23 in book 4. A problem map is a problem-solving enabling attribute that helps identify the best level on which to solve a problem. Problems can be dealt with at a fundamental root-cause level or at an overall organizational level. In a business context, for example, most every problem can be generalized up to the point of a profitability problem or dissected down to a human behavioral issue. You could either confront an issue like poor teamwork at an organizational profitability level by creating a team profitability incentive or at an individual behavioral level by coaching individuals on the finer points of collaboration.

The SCOPE of Leadership transcends the leadership problem map. It focuses on intrapersonal behavioral competencies at its foundation as well as broader organizational performance competencies at its top level. It provides a holistic perspective that enables leadership competence and performance at whatever level is most appropriate for a given situation.

People often engage me to help them with higher-level business and operational issues, but more often than not the root-cause issue that needs to be addressed is related to one of the lower-level competencies. The lower-level competencies in the SCOPE of Leadership get to the root of most leadership issues. Without them, attempts at leadership development and achieving exceptional results lack a reliable foundation. There isn't real depth of knowledge, understanding, or ability. Sustainable and deep competence only comes with a solid grounding in the basics.

The fact that leadership competencies depend upon each other and reinforce each other, combined with their intangible nature, makes learning leadership challenging. However, the SCOPE of Leadership uniquely organizes competencies and their enabling attributes into a straightforward model that makes the interdependencies and intangibles more tangible and understandable—as you are about to see.

FIVE CATEGORIES OF COMPETENCE

If there is one leadership quality that consistently stands out in great leaders, it is being engaged and action-oriented. Great leaders are constantly engaging themselves and those around them. When they attend meetings, they don't sit in the back corner so they can check their messages. They sit where they can listen, learn, contribute, and engage. They make their attendance count.

Neither do great leaders merely exchange superficial pleasantries when they meet people. They get to know people. They look for differentiating traits and unique capabilities. They seek others' wisdom. They look for common interests. They probe for opportunities. They make their interactions count.

> WHEN SOMEONE REQUESTS HELP OR NEEDS A DECISION TO BE MADE, GREAT LEADERS DON'T SIT ON THEIR REQUEST FOR DAYS OR WEEKS.

When someone requests help or needs a decision to be made, great leaders don't sit on their request for days or weeks. They make a decision. When a market opportunity arises, they capitalize on it. When they encounter a problem, they engage it rather than hope it will go away. They look for the upside in problems and how they can turn their challenges into opportunities. When they encounter a crisis, they take action immediately.

When great leaders make a trip, they get everything out of it they can. When they read a book, they find something in it they can use. Even when they play or take a vacation, they find opportunities to enhance their knowledge and fitness. They make their activities count, whether personal or professional.

Great leaders don't hold back. They take advantage of every experience. They leverage their resources and partnerships. They spot opportunities, make decisions, and execute. They are action-oriented. What you don't always see, though, is what enables them to make their decisions and take action.

There are five action-enabling categories of qualities possessed by action-oriented leaders. They are possessed by leaders at all levels who collectively make great organizations great. The categories start with the foundation category of basic competencies that build up to the advanced category of execution competencies. Each of these five categories and the competencies within them utilize the five TEMPT qualities as their enablers. Great organizations have great leaders who

1. Learn continuously, demonstrate competence, work intentionally, think strategically, possess courage, and set the example.

2. Communicate effectively, convey a positive attitude, promote trustworthiness, and motivate others to perform at their best.

3. Surround themselves with top-performing people, develop their people, enable them, and impart ownership to them.

4. Collaborate with others, leverage the synergy of teamwork, stimulate engagement, and build a climate of community.

5. Focus on value-adding activity, foster innovation, shape the culture, execute with excellence, and sustain high performance.

The SCOPE of Leadership framework is based on these five categories of qualities. The five categories spell out the acronym SCOPE. Each category builds on the one below it like layers in a pyramid as depicted in Figure 1.7.

Figure 1.7: The SCOPE of Leadership Pyramid

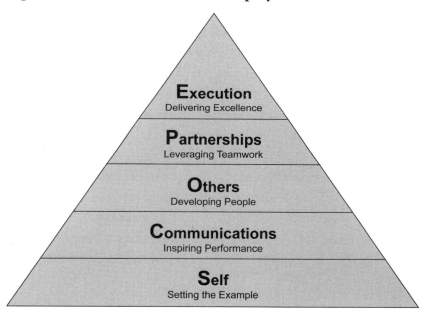

These five categories are the basis of the five remaining books of the SCOPE of Leadership book series. Including this book, the six books in the SCOPE of Leadership series are:

- Leadership Competencies That Enable Results
- Self: Setting the Example
- Communications: Inspiring Performance
- Others: Developing People
- Partnerships: Leveraging Teamwork
- Execution: Delivering Excellence

Enabling the five categories of the SCOPE of Leadership requires thirty-eight core competencies. These competencies are consistently found in great leaders regardless of the domain in which they work. The competencies are not aligned to any industry or particular role. These are competencies practiced by successful leaders around the globe in all industries, in all roles, and at all levels.

Given that leadership is about people, each category, or level, is associated with a particular group of people.

1. The foundation level is *self*. Great leaders lead themselves. They set the example for others to follow based on their own behaviors and attitude. *Self* is about building *intrapersonal* skills. The people of concern in the foundation level is one person—you. When thinking about this layer for yourself, it is the *me* layer.

2. The second level up in the leadership hierarchy is *communications*. Great leaders are great communicators. They move people to action through effective speaking, writing, and listening. They motivate and inspire others. *Communications* is about building *interpersonal* skills. In this layer, the focus turns from *me* to *we*.

3. The third and center level is about *others*. It contains the core of a coaching approach to leadership. It is a set of competencies focused on coaching, encouraging, and enabling others. *Others* focuses on developing people and holding them accountable. It is about imparting ownership to people. When you are thinking about this layer in terms of coaching someone else, you would refer to this as the *you* layer.

4. Level four is about *partnerships*. No one is successful on their own. Great leaders leverage others outside of their own team. They collaborate and partner with other people within their own company as well as with other companies. They foster

a climate of teamwork and community. They maintain high levels of engagement with their employees, suppliers, and partners. The competencies at this level are about how to work with *them*.

5. Level five is about *execution*. Great leaders execute and deliver exceptional results on a sustainable basis. They operate with excellence and continuously improve their organization. They maintain operational efficiency and quality. The competencies in this top layer leverage intra- and interorganizational capability to produce operational results. This is the *all of us* layer.

Within each of the five levels of the SCOPE of Leadership are specific competencies that enable the overall capability defined by that level. The foundation level that is focused on *self* is based on eleven competencies. The *communications* level contains seven competencies, the *others* level has seven, the *partnerships* level has six, and the *execution* level has seven. These make up the thirty-eight competencies exhibited by great leaders in the SCOPE of Leadership.

Within each of the thirty-eight competencies are key enabling attributes and subcompetencies. They are the attributes that enable you, or the people you coach, to develop that particular competency. The enabling attributes are the how-to building blocks for that particularly competency. They are attributes that anyone can learn and develop.

As you move down the pyramid from the top execution layer, the competencies are increasingly about individual professional development. As you move up the pyramid from the foundational basics, the competencies are increasingly about organizational development and operational execution.

From an external coaching perspective, the higher-level competencies are related to topics you would typically discuss with a *business coach*. The lower-level competencies are related to topics you would discuss with an expert on behavioral development, or in some cases a professional *psychologist*. Collectively, the thirty-eight competencies are related to topics you would discuss with an *executive coach*. This of course is a very general characterization, as many business coaches, executive coaches, psychologists, psychiatrists, life coaches, and consultants overlap each other and span different parts of the hierarchy of leadership competencies.

As you apply and incorporate the attributes of the lower-level competencies, the upper-level competencies come faster and easier. It is like learning the basics to any sport, musical instrument, foreign language, or other competency. Once you have the basics, you quickly progress to the more advanced levels. But when you try to perform at the higher levels without a grasp of the basics, you don't perform your best, if at all.

People who try to deliver results without having the underlying skills and competence to do so are like beginner skiers who go to the top of the mountain and try to immediately ski down an extreme slope without knowing how to turn or stop. Without the fundamentals, people are no better than amateur athletes trying to compete at a professional level for which they are not qualified.

If you attempt to lead a team of people without having the core underlying competencies, you won't be an effective leader. At best, you end up on the sidelines watching them do the best they can without you. Worse, you use brute force tactics, the power of your position, or your strengths regardless of their appropriateness for the situation. You end up forcing yourself on people using a *push* strategy. Because you don't lead by example, communicate effectively, know how to develop your people, or leverage team-work, you resort to pushing. You don't have the leadership skills of motivating, coaching, encouraging, or enabling, and so you try directing, telling, and coercing. You focus on accomplishing tasks instead of enabling and motivating people. If that doesn't work, you turn your attention to measurements, reports, and performance appraisals hoping the people will perform well on their own—none of which produces sustainable great results.

In contrast, managers who develop the competencies of the SCOPE of Leadership employ a *pull* approach to leadership. Their organization performs well because they are leaders who set an example that people want to follow. Their people have a leader who inspires them and motivates them. Their people have a leader who focuses on enabling them as individuals and as a team. Their leader pulls them into delivering results rather than pushing them. The people are more engaged, take more responsibility, and produce better results.

The effects of pulling versus pushing apply at home as well as work. Neither children nor spouses respond very well to being pushed. The SCOPE of Leadership competencies enable you to pull as well in your personal life as you will be able to in your professional life. The competencies are universally applicable. Once you learn them, you will apply them in whatever you do. Your intent in developing leadership competence may be to help yourself or someone else professionally, but you'll also improve yourself and them personally. When you are a true leader, you are a leader regardless of context.

The competencies and attributes in the SCOPE of Leadership are not new. I didn't invent them. Their roots are as old as the human race. I've merely pulled them together in one place, put them into a contemporary context, assembled them into a straightforward model, and made them easy to understand and develop. They are the product of my company's work, my own experience, and the insight gained from many great leaders.

The newness of these competencies for most people is the order in which they are presented, their enabling attributes, and the practical suggestions of how to apply them. Most seasoned managers know about them; they just don't necessarily apply them. This is why the SCOPE of Leadership book series emphasizes application.

Each of the chapters in the remaining five books of the SCOPE of Leadership book series is devoted to one of the thirty-eight competencies and its top eight enabling attributes. The attributes are the eight characteristics that I find to most often correlate with reaching the highest level of proficiency of that competency. The attributes represent the most recurring and salient themes for each competency.

Proficiency is dependent on many variables. In a typical brainstorming session on what contributes to a given competence, my clients and I routinely come up with ten to twenty different attributes. Of those, there are always several that differ among clients. The eight attributes listed for a given competency in the SCOPE of Leadership are the most important and foundational ones, but not all of the ones that might be needed in a specific situation. However, even the less frequent enabling attributes not included in one competency are included in other related competencies, providing you with a comprehensive understanding of all the enabling attributes you will need for most situations.

The reason for eight attributes per competency is that by the time you know the first eight enablers for most competencies, you have covered the most important ones. There are many attributes to enabling a competency, such as strategic thinking or fostering innovation, for example, but by the time you know the most important eight, you are well on your way to being a strategic thinker or facilitator of innovation.

Twenty-five of the enabling attributes repeat themselves in slightly different forms and contexts throughout the SCOPE of Leadership competencies. Their recurrence reveals the interdependencies that are part of leadership competence. I refer to these recurring attributes as the *Core 25*. As they repeatedly come up as enabling attributes in progressively advanced competencies, deeper insight into them is revealed. By the end of your reading of the SCOPE of Leadership book series, you will know these Core 25 attributes intimately well. Of these, just over half come from the first level of the SCOPE of Leadership: *Self.* They are part of the basics of leadership that form the underpinnings for nearly all of the leadership competencies. The *Core 25* are summarized in chapter 6 of this book.

The remaining books in the series include a self-assessment at the conclusion of each chapter to test your proficiency for each of the eight attributes for that leadership competency. These individual competency assessments are more detailed than the overall competency assessment provided in the next chapter of this book. Each individual competency assessment includes eight questions for each of the eight attributes a person needs to exhibit in order to be proficient in that competency. Use these chapter-ending assessments as your competency scorecard. I suggest you reassess yourself every year or so to monitor your progress in the competency attributes you are working on. Consider it your *leadership recertification test*. Also use the self-assessments to evaluate the leadership competence and potential of those you are coaching.

RECOGNIZING COMPETENCE

There are multiple approaches managers and leaders employ, as we reviewed in the section on leadership approaches in chapter 3. Leaders who lead as coaches emphasize the *coaching* approach. Leaders who lead as change agents emphasize the *transformer* approach. Coaches and transformers achieve outcomes through people who perform their best due to the leader's encouragement, inspiration, enablement, and coaching rather than through commanding, controlling, or doing. Like an athletic coach, they focus on building the attitudes, skills, and abilities of their people rather than simply telling them what to do.

The five categories of competencies in the SCOPE of Leadership emphasize the development of a coach and transformer approach to leadership. As you know now, both approaches heavily depend on the foundation level of setting the example, which focuses on the basics. As great coaches know, the basics are what differentiate a good player from a great player. Tony Dungy, the Super Bowl–winning coach of the Indianapolis Colts, said his championships were won by doing the ordinary things better than everyone else—day in and day out.

Managers who don't focus on the basics typically focus instead on the numbers. Rather than have their people learning, developing, and practicing the basics, they have them collecting, formatting, tweaking, and reviewing their numbers. In contrast, leaders as coaches and transformers reinforce the basics because they know you don't get results by focusing on the results but rather by focusing on that which produces results.

> MANAGERS WHO DON'T FOCUS ON THE BASICS TYPICALLY FOCUS INSTEAD ON THE NUMBERS.

You can spot the leaders who are coaches versus those who are managers by comparing them to the concluding competency at the end of each of the five levels in the SCOPE of Leadership, which represents the capability most necessary and representative of a leader as a coach for that level. For example, you recognize people who are great at the basics by their confidence, the concluding competency at the end of the first level and the foundation of the pyramid: *Self*.

The second level of the SCOPE of Leadership on effective communications focuses on inspiring and motivating people to action. It emphasizes building great content and delivery skills to enable you to pull people into action instead of pushing them. It is in contrast to managers with undeveloped communications skills who resort to telling their people what to do. Ineffective communicators don't have the ability to listen and motivate, so they resort to the brute force of commanding people what to do. Leaders as coaches motivate and inspire their team to levels of performance that come from intrinsic motivation rather than external coercion. You recognize teams led by leaders who are effective communicators by people's level of motivation, the focus of the concluding competence at the end of the second level: *Communications*.

The third level on developing others gets to the core of a coaching approach to leadership. It focuses on developing people's attitudes and abilities. It involves getting to know people as individuals and coaching them on how to leverage their abilities and overcome their shortcomings. Leaders as coaches exhort their people to rise to higher levels of performance than they could on their own. They impart ownership to their people and enable their people with tools and information. They encourage their people when they perform and hold them accountable when they don't. You recognize teams led by leaders who focus on developing others by the level of ownership their people take, which is the focus of the concluding competence at the end of the third level: *Others*.

The fourth level on leveraging partnerships is about working as a team. It is leveraging the synergy of diverse people with different skills in different roles and often from different organizations. It is about working fluently and in alignment with others. It is about overcoming differences of opinion, pulling together as one team, and having a team identity rather than a collection of individual identities. Leaders as coaches lead teams, not collections of individuals. You recognize teams led by leaders as coaches by their level of collaboration, which is the focus of the concluding competence at the end of the fourth level: *Partnerships*.

The fifth level of execution and the peak of the pyramid is about delivering excellence. It is about putting all the ingredients of great leadership together to create a high-performing team that produces exceptional results. It is about how to work through people, focus on value-adding activity, execute with excellence, and create competitive differentiation. It is about taking prudent risks and making great decisions. It is in contrast to managers who turn in inconsistent performances and create more *busyness* than *business*. Leaders as coaches produce consistently high results because they possess these higher-level competencies that include shaping the culture, fostering a climate of innovation, and enabling speed and quality. You recognize leaders as coaches who deliver excellence not only by their results but also by their action orientation and sacrifice, the focus of the two concluding competencies at this peak level of leadership competencies: *Execution*.

Each level of the pyramid also starts out with the foundation competency required for that level. To lead yourself effectively and set the example, you need to believe in what you do and the competency of *believing with passion*, the first competency in the foundation level. To communicate effectively, you first need the competency of *conveying a positive attitude*. To develop others effectively, you first need talent to work with and the competency of *attracting top talent*. To leverage partners and teamwork effectively, you first need to get out and meet people, build relationships, and the competency of *socializing for synergy*. To deliver excellence effectively, you first need the competency of *focusing on value*.

MINDSET AND ABILITY

Every action has two parts—an intention and a resulting effect. Every action (the *what*) is the result of a mindset (the *why*) and ability (the *how*). Behind every physical effort is a mental one. There is always a will and skill or an attitude and aptitude involved. Leading and developing people are no different.

Great leaders look below the surface of their people's performance to find their people's underlying attitudes and aptitudes. Great leaders coach and evaluate their people on both skill and will. Leaders achieve results and improve people's performance by working on people's mindset as well as their ability. Like athletes, people need not only a good technique but also the mental fitness to apply their technique, especially when in difficult circumstances. Stress, fear, and self-limiting thinking—when not properly dealt with—prevent people from performing even when they have the ability to perform.

Leadership is both a mindset and ability. The SCOPE of Leadership is therefore based on attributes that are a blend of attitudes and aptitudes. As you will discover in most chapters, the first attribute that enables a competency is a mindset. In some cases, so are the second, third, and fourth attributes. Particularly in the foundational level of Self, the basic competencies depend heavily on having the right mindset.

Both developing and properly applying a competency depend on having a proper mindset. Competence is preceded by a mindset, which is followed by application, which creates ability. Without the right frame of mind and application, ability doesn't develop. A gung-ho mindset without application is a dream. Conversely, rigorous application without the right attitude is activity without a purpose, or as I like to call it, *busyness as usual.*

> WITHOUT THE RIGHT FRAME OF MIND AND APPLICATION, ABILITY DOESN'T DEVELOP.

To give this some context in your work environment, think about your organization's core values. How many are mindsets versus abilities? If you're like most people, you've not thought about your core values in terms of these two categories. When you do, though, you'll realize your values are a mix of mindsets and abilities. You may not order them in a hierarchy, but if you look at them, you will realize the values that are mindsets logically precede the values that are abilities. As causes precede effects, mindsets precede abilities.

Your actions are the result of your thinking. To promote or develop a desired behavior optimally, you start with the mindset. If you want to optimally develop the ability to work more productively, for example, you start with its enabling mindset—a sense of urgency. If you expect to develop the ability to learn continuously, you need a degree of humility, its preceding mindset. If you expect to have the ability to innovate, you need a foundation mindset of curiosity.

Using the ten elements in the *genetics to results* continuum from chapter 3, here is another example starting with the same genetic beginnings but with a very different result due to a simple shift in mindset.

Genetic Expression (Level 4 Change):

1. **Genes and nurturing**—Your DNA and RNA combine with your childhood experience of playing math games and growing up on a steady diet of wild salmon, cacao beans, and green tea.

2. **Gene expression**—You develop a left-brain logical orientation and attend engineering school, which brings out your aptitude for analytical thinking.

Unconscious Thought, Deeply Held Values, and Instincts (Level 3 Change):

3. **Belief**—Your inner voice says, "I believe value in society is created through technological improvements."

4. **Principle**—You make decisions based on the underlying principle to solve any problem you find through the application of technology.

Conscious Thought (Level 2 Change):

5. **Goal**—You set a goal: "I'm going to produce the industry's most sophisticated new technology."

6. **Thought**—You think, "I'm going to design a prototype."

7. **Attitude**—You form the attitude, "I want my boss to be impressed by how quickly we can build a prototype."

Behaviors (Level 1 Change):

8. **Behavior**—You push your team hard to meet the prototype deadline.

9. **Habit**—You make tasks and deadlines higher priorities than people and relationships.

10. **Results**—You have poor relationships.

In this example, what was most observable? A casual observer might see only the poor relationships, but people on the team would see the behaviors that caused the poor relationships. Yet the pushy behavior still wasn't the root cause of the problem. The root of the problem was the mindset that preceded the behavior. The deviation in this example from the prior one in chapter 3 occurred at steps 5, 6, and 7—the person's conscious thinking. It could have also been the person's unconscious thinking. People's preceding thoughts, beliefs, principles, goals, and attitudes are the cause of their behaviors.

Effectively developing leadership competency, coaching your team, raising your children, selling, making presentations, winning votes from your constituents, and delivering peak performance through people all start with a mindset that is followed by an action. Learning the difference between the two and putting them in the right order is one of the most powerful leadership principles to understand. When people ask me for the single most important leadership principle they should understand, this is the one I share with them.

As a test of your understanding, if you wanted to improve your ability to confront conflict, would you start out learning the key steps to engaging in constructive debate? No, you wouldn't—not if you truly wanted to build your ability to constructively engage in conflict. Engaging in a dialogue is an ability. Learning starts with a mindset. The enabling mindset that precedes engaging in constructive conflict is openness to debate—having an open mind.

Unless you uniquely have the right mindset and simply lack the required knowledge, then knowing the action steps to any competency is insufficient. If you are like most people, the reason that you've not yet developed a competency is because you've not developed the right mindset. If you've been reluctant to confront an employee's poor performance, your reluctance probably isn't rooted in a lack of knowledge. Your issue isn't in not knowing how to hold people accountable. Your reluctance is rooted in a fear of reprisal, a lack of self-confidence, or your inability to get past your desire to have everyone be your friend. To reliably build your skill in holding people accountable, first you have to build your mindset of accepting that it is all right to be assertive—the constructive type of assertiveness, that is. Establishing the right mindset before building skill is a critical coaching competency that will be explained further in competency 21 in book 4.

Mindsets are powerful not only because they precede a specific behavior but also because they unconsciously reinforce multiple abilities. Unlike abilities that are more dependent on a specific context, mindsets are broadly applicable and support many behaviors. For example, having the mindset that you believe you can do anything enables you to engage in a broad range of activities, whereas a specific skill like the ability to replace vacuum tubes in antique television sets has limited applicability.

For a more in-depth understanding of developing mindsets and abilities, see my book *Activating Your Ambition: A Guide to Coaching the Best Out of Yourself and Others* (www.ActivatingYourAmbition. com).

PRINCIPLES VERSUS TACTICS

Great leadership isn't the application of tactics. It is the adoption and application of principles. Leaders don't memorize scripts, procedures, and techniques. They learn, cultivate, apply, and lead through principles. Tactics are very specific, only being useful in limited situations. Principles are broader, giving leaders the ability to apply them in many situations.

Principles are like geometry proofs. I remember struggling to learn them in high school, but when I finally did and I truly understood them, they made geometry much easier. Leadership principles are as powerful for leading people as geometry proofs are for solving geometry problems. They guide and direct you in solving many different problems and making many types of decisions. Where tactics are like answers to a specific math problem, principles provide a deeper understanding of how to frame and solve many problems. They take a little more work to understand, but when you do they are significantly more powerful than tactics.

In math, there is generally only one right answer. In much of science, there are only right or wrong answers. Leadership isn't so simple—hence the reason leadership isn't thought of as a science. But like proofs in science, principles can be reliably applied to provide leadership guidance and solve organizational problems. Principles give scientific support to the art of leadership. Principles of leadership provide fundamental truths but allow for adaptation to the context of a situation. Principles are the proofs of business that make the intangibles of leadership more tangible. They are like having a leadership navigational system. They guide thinking and behavior. The understanding and application of principles bring the art and science of leadership together.

> PRINCIPLES GIVE SCIENTIFIC SUPPORT TO THE ART OF LEADERSHIP.

Principles simplify decision making because when you live and lead by principles, most of your decision-making work has already been done for you. You start your deliberation with reliable proofs that reduce the uncertainty of your situation and analysis. You apply straightforward principles that have already been tried and tested. You simply have to know which principle to use based on the context of the situation and then make your decision.

As you learn and apply principles, they become buried in your subconscious mind. Many of your decisions require no deliberation because you simply act on your subconsciously embedded principles. The principles become part of your instinct. You as well as others might think you've become a brilliant intellectual because your decision making has been noticeably enhanced. You might be brilliant, but your enhanced decision making is more from understanding and applying principles. This is a primary reason great leaders are decisive and able to give an appropriate answer to people's questions quickly and with relative ease.

Your unconscious mind operates thousands of times faster than your conscious mind. It is also the majority of your mind as it represents about 90 percent of your brain. Most of your brain's processing occurs outside of your awareness. By developing principles and allowing them to direct you from your subconscious, you are tapping into a much larger cognitive ability.

You can direct people to follow tactics or you can teach them to follow principles. Imagine that you are a software sales manager helping your sales representative with one of her top accounts. You might tell her to do the following:

- Take the chief information officer from your target account to lunch.
- Invite the president out to a ball game.
- Call the procurement manager to talk to him about his procurement policies.
- Send a basket of cookies to the department administrative assistant.

Did you notice whether these are tactics or principles? They are tactics. For the specific situation for which you were coaching your salesperson, these tactics might have been perfectly appropriate, but they might not be for other accounts. In other accounts, it may be people in other positions whom you want her to engage with, and in other ways. A better approach would be to coach your salesperson on the fundamental principle behind the tactics—build relationships with the key influencers in the account and understand their needs. Had you coached her on the underlying principle, she would have had a better understanding of what she needed to do in other situations.

When we enrolled my daughter Angela in youth soccer at the age of four, I volunteered to become a youth soccer coach. Initially all I knew about coaching soccer was the objective—get the ball in the net. Embarrassingly, I remember being on the sidelines early in my coaching career yelling at my players to stand here, then there, and then somewhere else. It wore me out, as it did them and their parents. It didn't help them learn the strategy of the game either.

Not until I started coaching my players on principles instead of directing them with tactics did they learn the strategy of the game and begin to play at a higher level. It also enabled me to stop coaching them from the sidelines during the game, which isn't the best time to be coaching. Our girls' soccer team went on to become league champions, and I'm proud to say my daughter went on to become a top-tier NCAA athlete.

Some organizations are heavily dependent on the execution of well-defined processes that are the equivalent of tactics. Retail and restaurant chains, for example, implement policies and procedures to maintain consistency in their brand and customer experience across all their stores. It is a necessary and beneficial part of running any business that is based on high-volume transactions.

Standardized processes have a downside, though. Like tactics, they hinder adaptation. When the restaurant's waitstaff and host are instructed to follow programmed scripts, their communication comes across as impersonal, if not insincere. Too much rigid programming removes the personal touch.

Strict adherence to procedures makes employees, partners, and customers feel mechanically processed. Policies that are too narrowly defined prevent people from using common sense, applying good judgment, and being creative. Policies on safety and compliance are necessary, but other areas can often be better served by establishing guiding principles rather than procedures.

In contrast to rigid procedures, principles allow people to retain flexibility within boundaries. Rather than have a hostess memorize a scripted greeting that comes across as impersonal, coaching her to use a principle would better enable her to deliver a pleasant greeting. It would allow her to use her own unique communication skills and observations, while ensuring it fits within the restaurant's intended customer experience.

Following principles focuses your mind on what is important. Thinking by principles gives you a solid anchor for the absolutes but flexibility to adapt where individual judgment and application are appropriate. When properly defined, principles focus you on the desired outcome as well as how to achieve the outcome. They guide you in finding the delicate balance between achieving the best result and achieving it in the best manner possible. Having a mental library of principles gives you a better frame of reference than does a memory full of inflexible tactics.

Principles also help you use good judgment when you are stressed or in an emotionally charged mood. Where a tactic might not adequately deal with a particular situation, leaving you with only your emotions to guide your decision, principles give you sound logic to lean on. Because principles apply broadly and become part of your subconscious, you are more likely to employ a principle appropriately in a challenging situation than an ill-chosen tactic or inappropriate emotional reaction.

Another valuable quality of principles is that they deepen communications and bring out mindsets. When you talk with someone, you communicate at many different levels, as will be explained through the enabling attribute of empathy in competency 17 in book 3. At the shallowest levels of communication you talk about people, tasks, facts, and events. At deeper levels you talk about values, beliefs, and principles. When you talk at the deeper levels, you uncover, understand, and influence people's mindsets.

When I'm coaching someone, particularly in the early stages of our work together, people generally focus on their operationally oriented problems. They want to discuss topics like their lack of employee engagement, the need for better teamwork, or improving the speed of execution. At this level of discussion their thinking centers on behaviors rather than the underlying mindsets that are driving the behaviors.

When the conversation turns to principles, however, real communication and progress start to occur. Talking in terms of principles reveals people's underlying thoughts and attitudes. Discussion of principles enables deeper levels of communication that enable deeper levels of thinking that enable changes in behaviors. Thinking and communicating in principles are powerful capabilities. Principles not only guide behaviors but also bring out and guide mindsets.

Great leaders learn and coach others based on principles, which is the reason the SCOPE of Leadership is based on principles. The competencies in the SCOPE of Leadership framework and their supporting attributes are principle-based. The more you understand them and bury them in your sub-conscious, the more they will instinctually guide you to think and behave in the same ways that great leaders do.

> GREAT LEADERS LEARN AND COACH OTHERS BASED ON PRINCIPLES.

Listed at the conclusion of each competency chapter are the key principles that enable the attributes for that competency. Ensure you understand, apply, and embed these principles into your daily mode of operation. Add other principles to the list that are appropriate for your specific circumstances. Identify the principles you and your team need to adopt that will promote the indisputable values and important behaviors your organization needs to follow.

LEADERSHIP COMPETENCY MODELS

A common topic of conversation with managers is the hiring and firing of employees. Most managers with more than about a dozen people on their team will have at least one person who isn't performing well and at least one position they need to fill. With such frequent hiring and firing activity, you would expect managers to utilize well-defined competency models to guide them in making their hiring decisions. Yet most do not.

As explained in more detail in competency 19 in book 4, an important tool managers should have in their tool belt is a list of the specific qualities and competencies their employees need to possess in order for them to adequately perform the duties of their positions. Competencies guide managers not only in the initial selection of their employees but also in ongoing employee performance evaluations. Competencies drive the content for coaching, training, and development programs. Competencies facilitate succession and career planning. Much of what a manager does that is related to employee development depends on having a framework of specific competencies to refer to. Yet many managers don't use competency frameworks and models. They instead hire, evaluate, and fire people based on subjective perceptions such as a person's likability and comparisons to themselves.

What managers need, particularly when filling a leadership position and coaching people into a leadership position, is a list of the leadership competencies that are required to excel in that position. A manager needs to know the specific mindsets and abilities that best enable employees to meet the expectations of their positions. They need a *competency model*. The SCOPE of Leadership framework is such a competency model.

The challenge for many organizations is in developing and maintaining a relevant competency model. Because leadership is inherently complex, leadership theory evolves, human resource practices change, and organizational requirements shift, competencies shift and change too. For example, a company needing to reinvent itself would place high importance on the ability to innovate, while a company that had completed its transformation might place higher importance on improving efficiency.

Compounding the challenge of keeping competency models current is the need for models to support multiple roles, departments, lines of business, and geographies. A competency model that works for one line of business may not be completely aligned with the needs of a different line of business. There is no single set of competencies or competency model that accommodates all people in all roles in all situations. The SCOPE of Leadership may come close for many organizations, but you should still expect to customize it to your specific situation and update it over time if you decide to use it.

While there may not be a single right competency model, there are many wrong ones. There are overly simplistic leadership models and scorecards that ignore critical competencies. There are overly complex models that make leadership confusing if not frustrating. There are models that contain redundancies and conflicts. There are many that are simply not very well thought out.

If you embark on developing your own competency model, Table 1.9 lists important points to consider that were used in developing the SCOPE of Leadership competency model.

TABLE 1.9: CONSIDERATIONS IN DEVELOPING COMPETENCY MODELS

1. **Principles Versus Tactics:** Leadership is about employing principles, not tactics. Tactics are specific applications of principles. The problem with specifying tactics and techniques is that they are limited in relevance to specific situations. They are not broadly applicable. Their inflexibility underutilizes people's strengths, style, personality, and natural abilities. Effective competency models specify the *what* rather than the detailed *how to*. Define principles that enable the flexibility to use the right approach for a given situation. Great leaders and successful people follow principles rather than memorize specific tactics—and so do effective leadership models.

2. **Definition of Success:** Leadership is about influence. It is about delivering results. It is not about making money or being the CEO. It could be for some, but for others achieving results is doing meaningful work or furthering a difference-making cause. Achievement is different for different people, cultures, and organizations. Leadership models should be careful about defining success too narrowly or including competencies that only support specific results.

3. **Management Versus Leadership:** People in management positions need both management and leadership competence. The senior-most leaders are usually not mired in the day-to-day details that stereotypical managers might be, but that doesn't mean leaders are focused only on vision and strategy. Successful leaders and leadership models have both management and leadership competencies. They include management competencies such as managing performance as well as leadership competencies such as thinking strategically.

4. **Practicality and Perspective:** On any given day, my team and I might be leadership coaches, trainers, consultants, speakers, writers, or practitioners. There is a significant difference in our content, approach, and style depending on the area of our focus. Most professions aren't this diversified, and therefore most professionals have a narrower perspective. An industry executive will have a view of what constitutes a leader that is very different from the views of a professor of behavioral science. If you are creating a model for a university environment, seek input and counsel from an academician. If you are building a model for use in a corporate environment, seek counsel from a successful industry veteran. If you want your leaders to be entertaining and inspiring, seek counsel from an entertainer or professional speaker. The backgrounds of the people developing your competency model will dramatically influence the competencies you select. Be aware that while leadership theories with all their paradoxes and counterintuitive postulations are very interesting, they are not necessarily grounded in reality or practicality.

5. **Interdependency:** There are many books, articles, and seminars on the core competencies of leadership. Some promote a few competencies. Some promote dozens. Jack Zenger has his. John C. Maxwell has his. Rudy Giuliani has his, as do Jim Kouzes and Barry Posner, Colin Powell, Jack Welch, Warren Bennis, John Wooden, and many others. The number of competencies is not that important. The competencies themselves are what are important, as are their interdependencies. It is too simplistic to promote competencies without understanding their linkages and dependencies. Competencies are not equal, nor do they stand in isolation.

6. **Order:** A part of interdependency is hierarchy. Effective leadership models take into consideration the hierarchy of competencies. Certain competencies need to be developed before others. When developing a leadership model, consider which competencies need to be developed first, in parallel, or after others. As with an athlete, don't expect people to develop advanced skills without having a solid foundation of the basics.

7. **Mindset Versus Ability:** Great leadership requires a blend of attitudes and aptitudes. Some competencies are mindsets while others are abilities. It is much easier to develop ability when you have the enabling mindset that precedes it. Some try to "fake it till they make it," but pretending is not a very dependable approach. Effective competency models include the attitudes necessary to create the abilities. Leadership requires character and behavior. Attitude and aptitude. Will and skill. Mindset and ability. Understanding and application.

Apply these modeling principles in the context of your specific environment to build your own leadership competency model. Create a model that is well suited to the uniqueness of your organization, products, and market. As a start, review the thirty-eight competencies of the SCOPE of Leadership and their enabling attributes. Rule out the ones that are not important in your environment. Rank the ones that remain in terms of relevance to achieving your organization's mission and values. Add any other competencies that need to be added. Put them in categories and in an order that make sense for you.

When you have a draft of your competency model, debate and challenge it. See how well it aligns to your vision and mission. See how well it supports your organization's values. Compare it to the competencies of your top performers. Compare it to your performance management metrics and system. Check for alignment with your desired culture and other aspects of your organizational ecosystem. Determine what needs to change and make adjustments either to the model or to the other parts of your organizational ecosystem as necessary.

READING THE SCOPE OF LEADERSHIP

People relate best to topics that are of immediate relevance to them. You won't be very interested in operational efficiency if you don't have an operation to manage, but you will be very interested in engaging an audience if you are about to make a presentation. The SCOPE of Leadership is written as a guide to allow you to go directly to individual chapters based on what is most relevant to you in any given situation. However, because individual competencies build on other competencies just as an athlete's advanced capabilities rely on basic capabilities, I suggest you read the book series initially in serial sequence. Then, when you come back in the future to any individual competency for reference, you will have the benefit of understanding its dependencies.

> HIGHER-LEVEL COMPETENCIES WILL SEEM WOEFULLY SIMPLIFIED IF YOU DO NOT UNDERSTAND THE ENABLING ATTRIBUTES OF THE COMPETENCIES ON WHICH THEY ARE BASED.

Beginning in the next book of the SCOPE of Leadership book series, each chapter describes a single leadership competency, with each successive competency building on the competency described in the preceding chapter. If on your first read-through you choose to skip to the chapters of most relevance to you, the higher-level competencies will seem woefully simplified if you do not understand the enabling attributes of the competencies on which they are based.

If you are working with someone to build their confidence, you may want to go directly to competency 11 in book 2. If your immediate interest is in giving powerful presentations, holding people accountable, or making great decisions, you'll be tempted to go directly to those chapters, too. However, to re-emphasize, you'll find that each of these competencies, as with any other, is built on the preceding competencies and their enabling attributes. If you want to understand and properly apply a given competency, first understand the competencies on which it is based.

You will find that each chapter is a concentrated short course covering the most useful ideas and valuable practices for that particular competency. Rather than provide a lengthy and in-depth treatment, each chapter only covers the key points you need to know and the eight primary enabling attributes to get you started quickly on your way to building that competency.

If you want a more in-depth understanding of a given competency, many chapters reference other authors and experts you can refer to. There are many excellent resources available from other authors, consultants, and coaches on most of the competencies in the SCOPE of Leadership. While I'm an author and proud to be one, I know that books alone don't make changes. People do. Utilize this book series as well as other people and resources as you make the journey of understanding and applying the principles of great leadership.

PRINCIPLES IN REVIEW

Here are key principles from this chapter to keep in mind.

- **Performance:** Peak performance requires competence, mental fitness, physical fitness, enabling resources, and the support of others.
- **The Basics:** Get the basics right before attempting higher-level skills and more advanced pursuits.
- **Take Action:** Make your time count. Get engaged and take action.
- **Mindset and Ability:** Every action is the result of two parts. Develop both the mindset and the ability, with the mindset typically preceding the ability.

- **Principles:** Learn and coach others in principles, not tactics.
- **Perspectives:** People possess different perspectives depending on their experience. Involve others in developing your competency model whose backgrounds are aligned to the outcomes you expect to achieve.

CHAPTER SIX

BUILDING A
LEADERSHIP ROADMAP

No one remains quite what he was when he recognizes himself.
—Thomas Mann

Great leaders are learners. They continually improve themselves, whether learning new competencies or refining old ones. They look for opportunities to gain and apply new knowledge. They seek feedback from others. They test out new methods, practices, and tools. They don't become complacent with the status quo. They strive to continue to improve themselves and those around them.

The following section provides a leadership assessment to assist you in knowing where to target your continuous improvement. The assessment will help you understand how well you currently perform against the SCOPE of Leadership's thirty-eight competencies of great leaders. Take it as objectively as you can. The results will guide you, your manager, or your coach in focusing your leadership development efforts.

THE SCOPE OF LEADERSHIP ASSESSMENT

To complete the SCOPE of Leadership assessment on the following pages in Table 1.10, first determine the role you will assess yourself against. It could be your current role or a desired future role. So as not to have any confusion about what you are assessing yourself against, make a notation at the top of the assessment of the role to which your assessment applies such as "Engineering Team Leader," "Executive VP of Finance," or "Sales Manager."

For each competency, put an "H" (High), "M" (Medium), or "L" (Low) in the "Importance" column to represent that competency's relevance and importance to you for the role you are assessing.

In the "Score" column, assess the extent to which you believe you possess the competency by giving yourself one of the following scores:

- A minus ("–") for competencies you lack
- A check ("✓") for competencies in which you perform adequately
- A plus ("+") for competencies in which you excel

You will also find a "Priority" column on the left side of the assessment. Don't concern yourself with that column at this point. You will return and prioritize your competencies after you complete and assess your scores.

You will see that the eight enabling attributes for each competency are provided in the assessment. They are for your future reference. Don't concern yourself with what they mean or their context for now. You will fully understand each attribute after you read the competency chapters in the remaining books of the series. When you come back and retake this assessment in the future, you can then assess yourself against not only the competencies but also their enabling attributes.

TABLE 1.10: THE SCOPE OF LEADERSHIP ASSESSMENT			
Priority (1, 2, 3)	**Competency for Role:** _____	**Importance (H, M, L)**	**Score (–, ✓, +)**
	For each of the thirty-eight competencies listed in the following five leadership categories, assess the extent to which you: [fill in this blank with each competency].		
	Self: Setting the Example (Book 2) **Leaders who lead themselves and set the example:**		
	1. **Believe with Passion**—Believe in the organizational mission with passion and embrace it with enthusiasm. **Enabling Attributes:** • Cause • Enthusiasm • Incentive • Hope • Belief • Experience • Visualization • Reinforcement		
	2. **Pursue Goals within a Vision**—Set and pursue realistic but challenging goals that are clearly linked to the long-term vision, the current strategy, and meaningful objectives. **Enabling Attributes:** • Vision • Approach Behavior • Goals • Balanced Perspective • Positive Outlook • Accountability • Connection • Challenge		
	3. **Learn Continuously**—Continually adapt, seek new ideas, and find opportunities to learn and improve. **Enabling Attributes:** • Humility • Time • Eagerness • Energy • Change • Others • Discipline • Application		

Priority (1, 2, 3)	Competency	Importance (H, M, L)	Score (–, ✓, +)
	4. Know Self—Seek feedback and have awareness of the impact that your attitude, words, and behaviors have on others. **Enabling Attributes:** • Self-Assurance • Receipt of Feedback • Desire to Improve • Assessments • Openness to Experience • Reflection • Feedback-Rich Climate • Insignificant Blind Spots		
	5. Demonstrate Honorable Character—Demonstrate honorable character, ethical values, integrity, and honesty. **Enabling Attributes:** • Sense of Responsibility • Organizational Values • Respect for Others • Authenticity • Humility • Integrity • Ethical Values • Self-Control		
	6. Maintain Mental Fitness—Maintain mental sharpness, physical energy, emotional stability, and a healthy level of stress. **Enabling Attributes:** • Self-Investment • Good Nutrition • Restful Sleep • Relaxation • Physical Fitness • Absence of Chronic Stress • Positive Emotions • Enriched Personal Life		

Priority (1, 2, 3)	Competency	Importance (H, M, L)	Score (–, ✓, +)
	7. **Operate Intentionally**—Take initiative, plan, prioritize, and focus disciplined effort on the most important activities. **Enabling Attributes:** <ul><li>Goals</li><li>Priorities</li><li>Self-Starting</li><li>Persistence</li></ul> <ul><li>Planning</li><li>Focus</li><li>Temporal Intelligence</li><li>Restraint</li></ul>		
	8. **Think Strategically**—Understand the broader environment, consider the best timing to take action, and foresee the implications of decisions. **Enabling Attributes:** <ul><li>Attentiveness</li><li>Temporal Intelligence</li><li>Eye for the Unseen</li><li>Guiding Principles</li></ul> <ul><li>The Big Picture</li><li>Simplification</li><li>Others</li><li>Experience</li></ul>		
	9. **Work Productively**—Work with a sense of urgency in an organized manner and accomplish a significant amount of work with a high degree of efficiency. **Enabling Attributes:** <ul><li>Sense of Urgency</li><li>Discipline</li><li>Effective Communications</li><li>Workflow Approach</li></ul> <ul><li>Energy</li><li>Tools</li><li>Overcoming Obstacles</li><li>Planning</li></ul>		

Priority (1, 2, 3)	Competency	Importance (H, M, L)	Score (–, ✓, +)
	10. Possess Courage—Have the courage to be bold, get out of the comfort zone, and take prudent risks. **Enabling Attributes:** • Motivation • Preparation • Self-Acceptance • Visualization • Discomfort • Contingencies • Reframing • Victories		
	11. Exude Confidence—Exude confidence by having the competence required for the position and a positive yet humble self-image. **Enabling Attributes:** • Positive Self-Image • Toughness • Locus of Control • Competence • Self-Control • Fans • Humility • Presence		
Communications: Inspiring Performance (Book 3) Leaders who effectively communicate and inspire performance:			
	12. Convey a Positive Attitude—Outwardly convey a positive can-do attitude, seeing issues as challenges to be engaged rather than obstacles that can't be overcome. **Enabling Attributes:** • Ownership • Impermanence • Self-Esteem • Forgiveness • Gratitude • Solution Focus • Positive Thoughts • Joy		

Priority (1, 2, 3)	Competency	Importance (H, M, L)	Score (−, ✓, +)
	13. Promote Trustworthiness—Create an unselfish environment where people trust each other, communicate openly, and do what they say. **Enabling Attributes:** • Conscientiousness • Information • Loyalty • Transparency • Unselfishness • Competence • Integrity • Consistency		
	14. Articulate the "Why"—Provide relevant context and a compelling reason that supports ideas and the need to take action. **Enabling Attributes:** • Vision • Mind and Heart • Confidence • Urgency • Motives • Benefits • Problem or Opportunity • Power of Story		
	15. Provide Compelling Content—Develop high-quality, interesting, relevant, and compelling content in written and verbal communications. **Enabling Attributes:** • Purpose • Examples • Design and Flow • Multimedia • Theme • Exercises • Balance of Detail • Research and Preparation		

Priority (1, 2, 3)	Competency	Importance (H, M, L)	Score (–, ✓, +)
	16. Engage the Audience—Communicate information in a way that connects with people and maintains their attention. **Enabling Attributes:** • Sincerity • Expression • Optimism • Humor • Preparation and Rehearsal • Setup • Variety • Interactivity		
	17. Listen Attentively—Listen with undivided attention, display empathy, and accurately understand what others communicate. **Enabling Attributes:** • Compassion • Inquiry • Availability • Empathy • Patience • Focus • Nonjudgment • Note-Taking		
	18. Motivate—Motivate others and bring out their intrinsic passion to achieve desired outcomes. **Enabling Attributes:** • Enthusiasm • Feasibility • Consequences • Involvement • Alignment of Outcomes • Resources and Activity • Hope and Encouragement • Symbols		

Priority (1, 2, 3)	Competency	Importance (H, M, L)	Score (−, ✓, +)
	Others: Developing People (Book 4) **Leaders who develop and enable others:**		
	19. Attract Top Talent—Attract, recruit, select, and hire top performers. **Enabling Attributes:** • People Focus • Fit • Competence • Advancement • Opportunity • Respect • Need • Offer		
	20. Know the Individual—Get to know people individually, care about them, and understand their capabilities. **Enabling Attributes:** • Helper Mentality • Relationship • Time and Attention • Understanding • Acceptance • Observation • Accessibility and Availability • Accurate Perspective		
	21. Coach—Mentor, coach, and assist people in their professional development. **Enabling Attributes:** • Competence • Approach • Willing Participant • Coachable Moments • Proper Expectations • Application • Root-Cause Understanding • Support and Accountability		

Priority (1, 2, 3)	Competency	Importance (H, M, L)	Score (−, ✓, +)
	22. Exhort and Praise—Recognize, encourage, and exhort people to utilize their capabilities, reach for higher goals, take on challenging assignments, and be the best they can be. **Enabling Attributes:** • Credibility • Courage • Self-Discovery • Opportunity • Substance • Encouragement • Belief • Recognition		
	23. Enable Performance—Provide people with the resources they require and enable them to productively perform their work. **Enabling Attributes:** • Servant Leadership • Problem Solving • Stewardship • Tools and Resources • Optimal Allocation • Facilitation • Best Practices • Wise Counsel		
	24. Manage Performance—Evaluate people's performance, hold them accountable to clear performance expectations, and take quick ethical action when performance expectations are not met. **Enabling Attributes:** • Known Abilities • Performance Measures • Role Fit • Evaluation and Feedback • Expectations • Documented Agreement • Composure • Action		

Priority (1, 2, 3)	Competency	Importance (H, M, L)	Score (−, ✓, +)
	25. Impart Ownership—Instill in people a sense of responsibility and pride of ownership by empowering them to perform work on their own to the extent they are capable. **Enabling Attributes:** • Purpose • Candor • Conscientiousness • Enablement • Risk and Reward • Confidence • Attention and Support • Empowerment		
	Partnerships: Leveraging Teamwork (Book 5) **Leaders who leverage partnerships and teamwork:**		
	26. Socialize for Synergy—Value, build, and maintain a diverse network of synergistic relationships across the organization, with external partners, and with external influencers. **Enabling Attributes:** • Partnering Mentality • Great First Impressions • Needs • Promotion and Publicity • Social Intelligence • Something to Give • Getting Out • Contact Maintenance		
	27. Create Alignment—Create alignment between the needs and interests of collaborating organizations, both internally and externally, to reach acceptable compromises and maintain harmony. **Enabling Attributes:** • External Perspective • Reciprocal Value • Likability • Resources • Understanding • Defined Roles • Compromise • Shared Accountability		

Priority (1, 2, 3)	Competency	Importance (H, M, L)	Score (−, ✓, +)
	28. Build Community—Facilitate teamwork, camaraderie, fun, and a spirit of unity causing people to be loyal to the team rather than being focused on their own agendas. **Enabling Attributes:** • Openness to Others • Effective Communications • Loyalty • Shared Experience • Interdependency • Common Identity • Contribution • Absence of Politics		
	29. Stimulate Engagement—Stimulate positive sentiments and vitality in people that make them want to stay in the organization, engage in their work, and give their best effort. **Enabling Attributes:** • Respect • Vitality • Organizational Pride • Accomplishment • Role Fit • Future Opportunity • Positive Buzz • Empowerment		
	30. Manage Conflict—Civilly engage in disagreement, manage conflict, and constructively resolve clashes between people. **Enabling Attributes:** • Openness to Debate • Dignity • Civility • Understanding • Clear Expectations • The "Golden Rule" • Listening • Resolution		

Priority (1, 2, 3)	Competency	Importance (H, M, L)	Score (−, ✓, +)
	31. Collaborate—Foster a spirit of cooperation, drive organizational communication flow, and work jointly with others as a team. **Enabling Attributes:** • Collaborative Mindset • Plans and Processes • Sponsorship • Cross-Functional Teamwork • Supportive Manager • Communication Flow • Resources • Unpretentious Exposure		
	**Execution: Delivering Excellence (Book 6)** **Leaders who execute and deliver exceptional results:**		
	32. Focus on Value—Direct effort, time, expenditures, and resources to activity that directly contributes value to the organization and achieves desired outcomes. **Enabling Attributes:** • Operational Focus • Activity Linkage to Results • Customer Perspective • Meeting Effectiveness • Roadmaps • Organizational Alignment • Effective Time Allocation • Knowing the Details		
	33. Foster a Climate of Innovation—Encourage innovation and create an environment that respects original ideas, creativity, prudent risk taking, and beneficial differentiation. **Enabling Attributes:** • Curiosity • Absence of Barriers • Risk Tolerance • Experimentation • Diversity • Mastery • Free Time • Challenge to the Status Quo		

Priority (1, 2, 3)	Competency	Importance (H, M, L)	Score (−, ✓, +)
	34. Enable Speed and Quality—Maximize quality and speed of execution by removing obstacles, utilizing assets, streamlining processes, optimizing systems, and maintaining operational excellence. **Enabling Attributes:** • Sense of Urgency • Agility • Improvement Mentality • Quality • Asset Utilization • Streamlined Processes • Upbeat Employee Sentiment • Profitable Execution		
	35. Make Great Decisions—Exercise good judgment, make timely decisions, manage decision-making biases, involve the right people, and properly evaluate the relevant alternatives. **Enabling Attributes:** • Competence • Openness • Principles and Values • Criteria • Involvement • Data and Instinct • Bias Awareness • Approach		
	36. Shape the Culture—Shape and cultivate the desired organizational values, philosophies, attitudes, and behaviors. **Enabling Attributes:** • Values • Change Management • Principles • Examples and Symbols • Standards • Opinion Leaders • Clarity • Traditions		

Priority (1, 2, 3)	Competency	Importance (H, M, L)	Score (−, ✓, +)
	37. Take Action—Swiftly implement decisions, take action, and engage in opportunities that utilize the organization's capabilities. **Enabling Attributes:** • Courage • Preparation • Confidence • Opportunities • Intentionality • Initiation • Time and Timing • Managing Procrastination		
	38. Make the Sacrifice—Sacrifice time and self-interests for the benefit of the team and organization's best interests. **Enabling Attributes:** • Commitment • Completion • Continuous Progress • Stewardship • Proper Use of Power • Engagement • Effort • Accountability		

When you've completed the assessment, interpret your scores. Assign a priority in the left column of each competency based on the level of importance you assigned it and the score you gave yourself. Give yourself a priority level 1 for the top-priority competencies that you need to focus on, 2 for the next lower-level priority competencies, and 3 for the remaining competencies deserving of your attention.

Top-priority areas for development are the competencies that you rated as high (H) in importance, yet you scored yourself as lacking (−) in competence. Put a "1" in the priority column for this combination of "H" and "−". Next, look for combinations of competencies you scored as high (H) in importance and adequate (✓) in competence, as well as those you scored as medium (M) in importance and lacking (−) in competence. Put a "2" in the priority column for these. For your

"3" priorities, select the competencies you rated as medium (M) in importance and as having adequate (✓) competence.

Here are the combinations of importance scores and competence scores with their respective priority:

Priority	"Importance" and "Score" Combinations
1	H and –
2	H and ✓, or M and –
3	M and ✓

THE DELTA ROADMAP

Based on the scores and priorities you recorded in the preceding SCOPE of Leadership assessment, identify the leadership competencies you plan to develop further. For as many as you have the time, energy, and resources to work on, create a *delta roadmap*, which is an action plan that closes the gap between where you are now and where you aspire to be. In each action plan, define the overall objective you expect to achieve. Define the enabling goal you need to reach to achieve your objective, whether a skill, attitude, or activity. Then list the tasks you need to complete and the activities you need to stop doing in order to reach your goal. You will find suggested activities to put into your delta roadmap in the competency chapters in the remaining books of this series for the competencies you plan to develop.

Figure 1.8 is an example delta roadmap. In addition to an action plan, it includes background information for future reference and a current status field for monitoring progress. Use the delta roadmap to monitor your own progress as well as to review progress with your manager or update your coach. Also have your employees use it to review their development progress with you. See www.AlpineLink.com for a blank version of the delta roadmap.

Figure 1.8: Delta Roadmap

Objective: Improve Employee Engagement to 80 percent by April 1

Enabling Goal: Empower my team to write their own proposals and job estimates

Not To-Do List:

Due:		
11/1	Stop doing my team's proposals and estimates	☐
10/31	Have incoming bids routed to team instead of me	☐
10/8	Stop telling my team what to do; seek their input	☐
10/4	Stop procrastinating about delegating bid responsibility	✓
10/18	Stop micromanaging every detail of my team's work	☐

To-Do List:

		Due:
☐	Turn bid responsibility over to team members	11/1
☐	Give each team member a practice bid to complete	10/15
☐	Train my team how to use estimating software	10/15
☐	Document job estimating guidelines	10/23
☐	Read Mike's book, *Activating Your Ambition*	11/30
☐	Announce my empowerment plan to my team	10/7
✓	Complete my delta roadmap	10/4

Current Status: I currently do all of the proposals and bids for my team

Background: I've been a construction area manager for two years. I was a project manager before. Since becoming area manager, I've done all my team's proposals and estimates. This has caused them to feel uninvolved, unappreciated, and incompetent. They want to be empowered with the authority to write their own proposals. They want to develop and own the job estimates for the projects they manage.

I started this delta roadmap on October 4, at which time I created an average of five estimates per week for my team.

LEADERSHIP DEVELOPMENT AS AN INITIATIVE

In addition to self-assessments and individual development road-maps, there are many other approaches and resources available to help you develop great leadership competence. They range from subscribing to periodic newsletters to attending extensive leadership development programs. They vary from reading books on your own or as part of a team book club to participating in company-wide initiatives. They include single learning methods such as self-directed learning as well as multiple learning methods that integrate classroom education, on-the-job training, special assignments, ongoing self-assessments, and professional coaching.

The simple and economical approaches are fine, but if you are developing many leaders, particularly in a large organization, more sophisticated approaches provide the highest impact. Having people participate in occasional training programs and reading books is better than doing nothing but significantly less than what best-in-class organizations provide. Building the highest levels of leadership competence requires the use of learning methods that encompass knowledge building, repeated practice, exposure, and on-the-job application.

If you are planning to establish a comprehensive leadership development initiative, here are the basic steps to keep in mind. Start by building a cross-functional team including the senior leaders and human resource professionals who will craft the initiative. With the team in place, define the leadership competencies your organization's leaders need to possess in order to execute your organization's vision, values, and strategy. Develop a competency model as described in the previous chapter that includes the mindsets and abilities people need to have.

With your competencies defined and aligned to your organization's goals, determine the learning approaches you plan to incorporate into your initiative. Determine the extent of classroom education, online training, coaching, assessments, special projects, and experiential learning you expect people to participate in.

Determine the proficiency levels people will need for the leadership roles they perform. Define the standards, qualifications, and expectations people need to reach.

Consider where your leadership development initiative impacts your human resource systems. Determine where you need to integrate your initiative with your talent management, performance appraisal, career development, and succession planning programs. Consider the impact on your employee selection process and job descriptions. Plan for any adjustments that need to be made to your measurements and incentives.

Build out the details of your leadership development curriculum. Determine the details of the programs, assignments, assessments, and learning methods you plan to use. Determine who will be teaching and coaching. Determine where and when the courses, projects, and activities will take place. For the period of time people will be participating in the initiative, define the schedule of events they will participate in.

With a defined curriculum in place that is integrated with your human resource processes and systems, select the people who will participate in it. Select the high-potential managers you expect to be part of the program. Make the program an exclusive opportunity that people aspire to participate in. Execute the initiative with excellence and monitor the results to ensure it meets the expectations you originally set. Make adjustments over time to ensure the initiative continues to meet the evolving needs of the organization.

PRINCIPLES IN REVIEW

Here are key principles from this chapter to keep in mind.

- **Assessments:** Assess your leadership competence every year or two to evaluate your progress in developing the competencies that you aspire to develop.
- **Development Priorities:** Establish your development priorities based on the combination of how competent

you are in a given competency and the importance of the competency to your role.

- **Delta Roadmaps:** For the competencies you plan to further develop, determine the enabling goals you will pursue to close the gap between where you are and where you aspire to be. Identify and track the actions you plan to take as well as the activities you plan to stop.
- **Leadership Initiatives:** If you are planning to establish an organizational leadership initiative, consider the sponsors, learning methods, HR systems, competencies, and participants that will be affected and should be involved.

CHAPTER SEVEN

CLOSING THOUGHTS

*What we think, or what we know, or what we believe is, in the
end, of little consequence. The only consequence is what we do.*

—John Ruskin

Leadership isn't about knowledge, intellect, or position. It doesn't matter where your name is on the organization chart. Most of the world's best inventions, most influential movements, and most important contributions to mankind did not come from people at the top of an organization chart.

What matters most and determines your success is not your position. It is your ability to deliver results with and through people. Your ability to leverage opportunities, overcome obstacles, and perform comes down to your ability to work with and influence people. As with an athletic coach, great leadership and performance come down to how well you coach people—both yourself and others—in the five enabling qualities of great athletic performance:

- Technique—knowledge, skills, and ability
- Equipment—systems, tools, and enabling resources
- Mental Fitness—attitude, mental toughness, and passion

- Physical Fitness—energy, endurance, strength, and effort
- Teamwork—collaboration, assistance, and synergy

These are the determining factors for achievement in any field, role, or position. They are the enablers to human performance improvement. They apply to you and everyone on your team. Having the ability to improve these capabilities is the essence of being a great leader and coach.

When you think about what prevents you or your team from delivering better results, consider that the issue is rooted in one of these five qualities of human performance. Yes, there might be process or system issues. The organization's incentives might be out of alignment with the organization's values and intended direction. Products, features, prices, and marketing approaches might need to be improved. There might be tight budgets, outdated policies, supply constraints, and a sluggish economy, but at the root of every issue are people. Supplies are constrained, products are outdated, processes are inefficient, and spending is tight because of people. If there is one ability that is most important to your success, it is your ability to work with and influence people. It is your ability to develop, improve, enable, and influence these five qualities of human performance. There are few issues you can't overcome by targeting one or more of these qualities.

The value of your leadership comes down to how well you enable these five qualities in yourself and the people within your circle of influence. As with a coach or athlete, these five qualities determine whether you win or lose. They determine how well you perform as a coach and help others perform.

To determine how well you lead, coach, and enable these qualities in the people within your circle of influence, reflect on these questions:

- Do the people in your circle of influence perform better by association with you?
- Do they feel encouraged and motivated by you?

- Do they have clarity of purpose and clear direction?
- Do they have the resources they need to perform their best?
- Are they skilled and knowledgeable?
- Do they possess the vitality needed for the work they perform?
- Is there good communication and collaboration between them?
- Do they execute with excellence?
- Do they consistently deliver top performance?

If you can't answer yes to these questions, I hope you will make it a goal to be able to do so soon. Take advantage of this opportunity to go to work on your leadership competence. Learn how to coach consistently and enable these five qualities of human competence and performance.

LET THE FIVE COMPETENCY AREAS DO THE WORK

Coach the five enabling qualities of great performance by developing the competencies within the five categories of the SCOPE of Leadership framework. Start by leading yourself. What your team does is the result of what you do, who you are, and the example you set. Believe in what you do with passion. Pursue goals that support the organization's vision. Continually invest in yourself. Demonstrate honorable character. Maintain your mental fitness. Operate intentionally and with discipline. Possess courage and maintain high self-esteem. Exude confidence that is grounded in competence and humility.

With a solid foundation of the basics in place, turn your attention to communication. How you communicate determines whether you motivate and encourage people or demotivate and discourage them. Convey a positive attitude. Promote trustworthiness. Provide compelling content. Engage your audience. Listen attentively and seek understanding. Leave people motivated and inspired.

With strong communication skills in place, focus on attracting capable people and developing them. Attract top talent. Get to know them individually and build their competence as you are building your own. Develop your successor. Create the future leaders who will build on your progress. Focus on developing your people, their skills, and their knowledge. Manage their performance and hold them accountable. Impart ownership to them.

In addition to developing your people, leverage others, partnerships, and teamwork. Develop collaborative, cross-functional relationships with other departments in your organization. Build a network of people who augment your knowledge, experience, abilities, scale, and relationships. Develop synergistic relationships with suppliers, customers, and business partners. Create alignment with your partners. Foster a spirit of community between members of your team and those with whom they work. Manage conflict so that disagreements are constructive differences of opinion rather than unconstructive arguments.

Pull all the elements of your organizational ecosystem together to turn your skills, knowledge, communications, employee capabilities, teamwork, and partnerships into exceptional results. Focus your team's efforts on value-adding activity. Foster a climate of innovation and build competitive differentiation. Manage biases and make great decisions. Take action. Create opportunities. Execute with speed and quality. Shape the culture.

These are the competencies and principles that make up the SCOPE of Leadership. Learn them, understand their enabling attributes, and put them to work. You will then possess the abilities of great leadership. You will be able to lead, coach, encourage, motivate, inspire, enable, and assimilate people into high-performing teams. You will be able to enable peak performance and results.

REALITY CHECK

While learning to become a great leader significantly enhances the odds of success for you and your team, don't expect perfection. Great leaders still have problems and encounter issues. As a great leader and coach, you will occasionally have bad days, if not bad quarters. You will make mistakes. You won't always be successful at everything you do. The more competent you are, the more action you will take and the more success you will have, but you'll also have more issues and mistakes, if not failures. Encountering issues is inevitable. It is part of being out front and being the leader.

Neither is success always within your control. You can be the best leader and coach a team could ever hope to have, but that doesn't prevent factors outside of your control from exerting their counteracting influences. No matter who you are and how good you are, there will be circumstances you didn't create or influence that will prevent you from making the difference you are capable of making.

There are market, social, economic, and political forces that make or break industries that leaders have no control over. There are hurricanes, tornadoes, and earthquakes that cause unforeseen disasters on a massive scale that you have no control over. Neither is it your fault that a market-crushing law is passed, the overall economy goes into a recession, or an entire society decides it prefers something new over something old.

This is not to say that you shouldn't continually try to adapt to the circumstances around you. As a great leader, you do continually adapt and find all reasonable ways to maintain a top-performing organization. You also continually try to influence your circumstances and improve them. To the extent you are able, you influence laws, markets, social norms, and economies. You also exercise patience and avoid taking actions that would negatively impact your circumstances. Yet despite all that you do as a leader, you encounter obstacles and issues you have no ability to control or influence.

As a leader, you also encounter people who won't change. Just because people can change doesn't mean they will. By no fault of yours, there will be people who won't accept your coaching, encouragement, facilitation, enablement, or assimilation. There will be people who resist your initiatives despite your best efforts. There will be people with fears and anxieties that they can't overcome. There will be people who have personality disorders, mental illnesses, and family problems that you can't affect.

The World Health Organization and the American Psychiatric Association are the primary organizations that define and maintain definitions of mental illnesses and disorders. Based on their definitions, studies find that more than one in three people have a mental illness or personality disorder of some type in their lifetime. As a leader and coach, realize that as good as you might be, many people have issues that you can't coach them out of. Even if you are a professional counselor, psychiatrist, or psychologist, there is no guarantee your efforts will help people overcome a mental illness. Like physical illnesses, mental illnesses are difficult to overcome and many have no cure. At best, many mental illnesses can be treated and managed.

> STUDIES FIND THAT MORE THAN ONE IN THREE PEOPLE HAVE A MENTAL ILLNESS OR PERSONALITY DISORDER OF SOME TYPE IN THEIR LIFETIME.

As a leader, you are in the business of encouraging, enabling, coaching, facilitating, informing, and assimilating people. Unless you are also a certified mental health professional, you are not a counselor. Don't expect that you can conquer everyone's issues. You might be able to offer everyone your encouragement and empathy, but it won't be enough to overcome everyone's issues. There will be mental illnesses and family issues, as well as tsunamis and droughts, you can't overcome. Do your best and strive for excellence, but be realistic. Realize people and circumstances won't always be what you want.

THE *CORE 25*

Part of the reality of leadership is that no one is a master of every attribute. There is too much to learn and do, and there is too little time to do it in. Jack Zenger, leadership expert and coauthor of *The Extraordinary Leader*, found that great leaders only had to demonstrate mastery in five of his sixteen top leadership competencies. In other words, he found that if you can master about a third of the competencies, you can still be a great leader. You need some degree of ability in the other competencies, but you don't have to master them.

Within the five levels of the SCOPE of Leadership, there are thirty-eight competencies. Each of these competencies is built on eight enabling attributes, adding up to a total of 304 attributes. If you were to master about a third of the attributes, that would be one hundred. It turns out, though, that you can be well on your way to becoming a great leader by mastering much fewer. Of the 304, there are twenty-five core attributes that are especially important. They show up repeatedly in slightly different forms, but each encompasses an especially important attitude or ability that enables multiple competencies.

These twenty-five attributes equate to about 8 percent of the total 304 attributes listed. I refer to these as the *Core 25*. These underpin many of the competencies consistently exhibited by great leaders. They include a combination of attitudes and aptitudes. They are listed in Table 1.11.

The *Core 25* deserve your primary attention. Review and emphasize them as you work on developing your leadership competence. Ensure they are well represented in your and your team's delta roadmaps.

These twenty-five attributes enable most of the competencies of great leadership. If you embody and perform these, you are almost guaranteed to possess the competencies needed to be a great leader.

Table 1.11: The *Core 25* Attributes

- Integrity
- Confidence and self-esteem
- Humility and openness
- Positive can-do attitude
- Vitality and energy
- Experience and competence
- Enabling tools, resources
- Respect for others, unselfishness
- Courage to leave comfort zone
- Interest in learning, developing
- Guiding principles and values
- Accountability and consequences
- Symbols, examples, stories

- Involvement of others
- Clear expectations
- Preparation and planning
- Problem-solving skill
- Temporal intelligence
- Customer perspective
- Articulation of the "why"
- Purpose and goal orientation
- Interdependency, support team
- Listening, seeking to understand
- Discipline, persistence, focus
- Empowerment, opportunity

It is a gross oversimplification, but you can reduce most of these attributes to seven themes: *Get up, grow up, team up, set up, show up, serve up,* and *don't give up*. These seven themes embody the essence of leadership and success in general. You have to get up, decide to do something, and set a goal. You have to grow up, gain experience, develop yourself, and build your confidence. You need to team up, leverage others, and work as a collaborative group. You have to set up, plan, and prepare. You have to show up, be proactive, create the opportunity, and turn your desire into action. You need to serve up the needed resources, provide motivation, give assistance, and focus on others. You have to persist, not give up, and not let problems stop you from reaching your goal.

> GET UP, GROW UP, TEAM UP, SET UP, SHOW UP, SERVE UP, AND DON'T GIVE UP.

If you and everyone on your team demonstrate these seven themes and twenty-five attributes, most everything else takes care of itself. You'll find learning and applying the thirty-eight competencies of great leadership as simple and straightforward as taking a stroll through the park.

Make the *Core 25* your top priorities as you build your leadership competence and that of those whom you lead. The advanced competencies in the higher levels of the SCOPE of Leadership framework will come easily if you simply focus on their root enablers, the majority of which are embodied by the *Core 25*.

DON'T LET YOUR EXPERIENCE BE CONCEPTUAL

Once you've read all six books in the SCOPE of Leadership series, you will know exactly what to do and how to do it. You will have made a sizable investment in time. At that point, if not well before then, expect to obtain a return on your investment. Plan to put your knowledge into practice and make your investment more than an academic exercise. Prepare to make some changes, as you will be turning your attention from knowing to doing.

Many people keep doing the same activities day after day even though their activities aren't working for them. They are running as fast as they can on the treadmill of busyness as usual but not making any real progress in their career or life. Instead they are stressing out and burning out. If you are one of them, take this opportunity to make a significant change. Try a new approach. Make the decision to get off the treadmill. Decide to lead instead of do. Plan to put your talents, skills, and knowledge to work as a great leader instead of a supercontributor, taskmaster, or organizer. Commit to learning the competencies of a great coach and transformer. Commit to making real change in the areas you need to change in order to become a great leader.

Stop now and make your plan. While this book is still fresh on your mind, make a list of your top takeaways. Review your SCOPE of Leadership assessment results from the previous chapter. Determine which competencies are most important for you in your role. Note the areas in which you are highly capable that you need to continue to leverage. Identify the competencies you are not as capable in and plan to develop further. Know which competencies to give particular attention to as you get to them in the next five books of the series.

Think about your learning approach. Decide if you will establish a book club. If there are others in your circle of influence who share your interests in leadership, form a book club. Recruit your colleagues, friends, or neighbors to join your book club. Take advantage of not only this book series but also the many other great books that are available. Great leaders are learners and learners are readers.

Think about seeking a mentor or recruiting your boss to be your coach. Think about whom you might seek feedback from to help confirm the areas in which you need to develop. Consider who might be an accountability partner to hold you accountable to becoming a better leader. Consider whether you should take a 360 assessment, investigate more formal training programs, or hire an outside coach. A seasoned executive coach will help you focus on the specific areas you need to work on in order to be the best leader you can be. Coaches can be great facilitators of your development as well as sources of wisdom, encouragement, and accountability. Great coaches help you learn as well as put your knowledge into application.

If you are like most leaders I coach, you will have to resist the natural tendency to keep doing what you've always been doing. You will need to endure a little discomfort for a few days and weeks as you adopt new attitudes and try new behaviors. Stay with it, though, and before you know it you will have developed new habits. You will have developed the competencies of a great leader. Change doesn't take that much time. It just takes disciplined effort. It requires that you make your experience real rather than let it be conceptual.

If you are reading this book as part of a leadership development program, think about who made this program possible. Thank them for giving you this opportunity. If you already completed a 360 assessment as part of the program, also thank your feedback providers. Let them know what you plan to do with their feedback. They will appreciate your gratitude.

LEAVE A LEGACY

Have you ever thought about how you want to be remembered in your role, your organization, or your life? Do you want people to describe their memories of you in a particular way? What words do you hope they use? Take a few minutes and write down ten words you hope people use to describe you. Are they words like honest, compassionate, exhorter, coach, or leader? Are they the same words that people would actually use today based on who you are now? Or are they words you merely wish people would use?

As you think about your leadership development plan, think about how you want to be remembered. Consider how well you currently exemplify the characteristics you want to be remembered by. Emphasize in your development plan any changes you need to make to be the person you want to be remembered as.

If there is one consideration that motivates people to do something more than any other, it is their reputation. Your reputation embodies your core identity including your trustworthiness and competence. Consider the value and importance of leaving a legacy as a great leader and being remembered for your great leadership.

Studies based on employee, citizen, and stakeholder opinions find that there is about a 75 percent chance that you are not a great leader. Unless this book appeals only to the top quartile of leaders, chances are high that you are more focused on projects, tasks, systems, machines, presentations, reports, compliance, results, or perks than people. If you are, realize that your spreadsheets, charts, tools, and processes won't remember you but your people will. Your people are the most important assets you have and the most deserving of your great leadership.

> STUDIES BASED ON EMPLOYEE, CITIZEN, AND STAKEHOLDER OPINIONS FIND THAT THERE IS ABOUT A 75 PERCENT CHANCE THAT YOU ARE NOT A GREAT LEADER.

If you don't already focus on people, start now. Turn your attention to people. Stop working on your presentation or spreadsheet. Stop writing the report or proposal you are working on. Stop focusing on equipment, systems, projects, and tasks at the expense of your people. Get out of your chair and go work with your people. Make them your top priority. Stop controlling and start coaching. Stop telling and start inspiring. Enable your people to create the presentations, write the proposals, manage the projects, and complete the tasks. Take the focus off of yourself and put it on your team. Make coaching, encouraging, leading, enabling, and assimilating them your primary focus.

No one in their final days wants to have their accomplishments at their bedside. They want their closest coworkers, friends, and family. Don't let your life be consumed with busyness and mindless tactical execution at the expense of building and nurturing people. Become the inspiring leader who makes everyone around you better by simply being around you. You will be cherished and respected, and you will also deliver results like never before.

If you want to be remembered for being a great leader, you can be. It is up to you.

THERE ARE NO EXCUSES

The thirty-eight competencies in the SCOPE of Leadership are all within your control. They are all within your ability to learn and apply. For the most part, they don't cost any money or require any substantial resource other than your time and effort. You don't need a budget, staff, or approval to move forward. You don't need anything but the will to take action. You control the decision to become a great leader.

If you currently work in an environment that accepts mediocrity, realize that you don't have to accept it. You can rise above it. Don't let your circumstances or others define you. Don't let others tell you what you can or can't do in terms of your abilities. Don't let the people around you discourage you.

Make a list of any obstacles that are preventing you from developing your leadership competence to a higher level. List the people who are getting in your way. List the urgent yet unimportant activities that are taking up your discretionary time. Identify any unnecessary tasks or unproductive work preventing you from turning your attention to developing your leadership ability. Identify any needed yet unavailable resources holding you back. Record everything that is getting in your way of becoming a great leader.

If you are like most people, there are probably a number of items on your list. When you look at them collectively, they might seem overwhelming. You might be too tired to fight another battle or start another initiative. You probably have little time but much to do. If this resonates with you, realize that the reason you can't improve your leadership is that you lack the time and energy, which is the result of issues that could be prevented—if you only improved your leadership. You might not be able to see it in yourself, but realize that the reason most people don't have the time and energy to change is due to the very changes they need to make.

If you are stuck in a cycle you can't seem to stop, break out of it. Push aside the excuses. Be honest with yourself. You are gaining nothing by staying in the rut of busyness as usual. Take charge of your future. Invest in yourself. Make time to learn and develop. You will start becoming a great leader as soon as you stop perpetuating your problems and start solving them.

ENHANCE YOUR SIGNIFICANCE

In a typical financial analysis, the value of an investment takes into consideration not only its current value but also its future cash flows and future value. Similarly, your current net worth is based not only on your current worth but also on your future ability to add and create value. Your net worth is based on your capacity to make a positive contribution in the future.

Consider the investment in your skills and leadership competence as an investment that will provide a tangible return. It will significantly increase your net worth. Leading people is a high-value activity. The better you are able to coach, motivate, influence, develop, and assimilate people, the more valuable you are and the higher your net worth will be. The more ability you have to create value through others, the more value you will create in the world and for yourself. Consider that the intangible qualities of leadership may be worth more to you than your college degree, investment property, or current retirement account. The extent to which you can create value and lead others to create value determines how important and significant you are.

Your leadership value is based on how well you possess and enable in others the competencies of the SCOPE of Leadership. If not your current employer, a potential future employer will highly compensate you for these qualities.

At the risk of confusing you with one more model and acronym, I've put the competencies on which the SCOPE of Leadership is based as well as the more commonly referenced enablers of increasing your net worth in the form of an acronym that spells out the word *significance*, as shown in Table 1.12.

TABLE 1.12: FACTORS THAT DETERMINE YOUR TRUE NET WORTH

S—Skills, abilities

I—Information, knowledge

G—Guarantee, commitment, faith

N—Network, relationships

I—Inner drive, passion

F—Financial resources, assets, creditworthiness

I—Integrity, honesty

C—Conscientiousness, concern for others

A—Ability to learn, mental capacity

N—Nature, attitude

C—Conditioning, health, longevity

E—Experience, record of accomplishments

These are the attributes and qualities that determine your true financial net worth and significance. These are the characteristics that people will pay you for. As you will see, most are also the characteristics that enable you to be a great leader.

If making money and increasing your net worth is a goal for you, make these areas your focus. Give them your continued investment and they will give you a continued return.

You now have several models: this *significance* model, the *Core 25*, the seven themes, the thirty-eight competencies in the SCOPE of Leadership, the TEMPT model, the six approaches to leadership, and the four levels of change between genetics and results. I hope these models along with the other content in this book have made you think in some new ways about what you can do to become a better leader. I hope you see that through understanding and applying this material, you can expect your leadership competence, attitude, energy, productivity, earnings, and net worth to grow.

THREE THOUGHTS

If I could leave you with only three thoughts, they are these:

1. **Seize the opportunity.** You can do anything you put your mind to. Don't let fear or other obstacles prevent you from becoming your best. It benefits you and everyone you influence, including your family, friends, and coworkers. Break out of the tyranny of the urgent. Focus on what is important. Make developing your leadership skills your top priority.

2. **Rise above mediocrity.** It seems that cultural norms continue to set new lows. People continue to find new ways to take the easy way out. Standards of performance, accountability, and responsibility continue to decline. Don't buy into the herd mentality. Rise above it. Don't settle for mediocrity. There are times to follow, and then there are times to lead. When the people around you are living and working by mediocre standards, it's time to lead.

3. **Pass it on to others.** Life is about relationships. It is about making a positive difference in the lives of others. Turn your focus to people. Give where others take. Your investment will not only produce the results you have been working so hard to create, they will come back to you personally with interest. Emerging leaders need the help of seasoned leaders. Every organization needs coaches. If you are a seasoned leader with an aptitude for coaching, pass it on to others. Your unique blend of experience and coaching skill makes you a valuable resource.

GET SERIOUS

In closing out this first book of the SCOPE of Leadership series, I hope you take the need and opportunity to lead seriously. If you were not already serious about improving your leadership competence, or that of your team, I hope you are now. The world needs your leadership. There is a leadership crisis among us, and we can't all hope that someone else steps up to fill the gap.

If you know what you need to do to be the best leader you can be, great. Go do it. Go lead. Think, communicate, and behave in a way that makes a substantial and positive difference in your circle of influence. Coach, enable, and inspire others to be their best.

If you are unsure how to lead or of the best next steps to take, seek wise counsel from someone you trust who is in a leadership position. Talk to your manager, your board, a trusted friend, a parent, or your spouse. If looking foolish is a concern, stop worrying about it. Other people already know you're not perfect. Neither are they—whether your boss, employees, or peers. Have the courage to suggest that there is a need for leadership and that you're willing to take on the responsibility.

Allow yourself to be vulnerable. Be bold. Break out of your comfort zone. Whatever you need to do to improve your leadership ability that is within the realm of feasibility and reasonability, do it. Leadership is exciting. Being in a position of influence is rewarding. Enjoy your leadership development opportunity. Embrace the SCOPE of Leadership and become a great leader.

Best of luck,
Mike Hawkins

APPENDIX

THE SCOPE OF LEADERSHIP SCORECARD

Complete the following scorecard in Table 1.13 as you finish each competency chapter in the next five books of the series. When you have completed the scorecard, compare these results to how you first assessed yourself in chapter 6. Note where your increased level of understanding in any given competency has changed your scores.

To score yourself, put a check mark in the "Importance" column for each competency that is important to your current role or future desired role. If you want to be more specific, write an "H" (High), "M" (Medium), or "L" (Low) to represent that competency's relevance and importance.

In the "Score" column, give yourself one of the following scores for each competency:

- "–" for competencies with more of the enabling attributes scoring minuses than pluses
- "✓" for competencies with an equal number of the enabling attributes receiving minuses and pluses
- "+" for competencies with more enabling attributes scoring pluses than minuses

Priority (1, 2, 3)	Competency for Role: _____	Importance (H, M, L)	Score (-, ✓, +)
TABLE 1.13: THE SCOPE OF LEADERSHIP SCORECARD			
Self—leaders who lead themselves and set the example:			
	1. Believe with Passion		
	2. Pursue Goals within a Vision		
	3. Learn Continuously		
	4. Know Self		
	5. Demonstrate Honorable Character		
	6. Maintain Mental Fitness		
	7. Operate Intentionally		
	8. Think Strategically		
	9. Work Productively		
	10. Possess Courage		
	11. Exude Confidence		
Communications—leaders who effectively communicate and inspire performance:			
	12. Convey a Positive Attitude		
	13. Promote Trustworthiness		
	14. Articulate the "Why"		
	15. Provide Compelling Content		
	16. Engage the Audience		
	17. Listen Attentively		
	18. Motivate		
Others—leaders who develop, coach, and enable others:			
	19. Attract Top Talent		
	20. Know the Individual		
	21. Coach		
	22. Exhort and Praise		

Priority (1, 2, 3)	Competency	Importance (H, M, L)	Score (–, ✓, +)
	23. Enable Performance		
	24. Manage Performance		
	25. Impart Ownership		
Partnerships—leaders who leverage partners and teamwork:			
	26. Socialize for Synergy		
	27. Create Alignment		
	28. Build Community		
	29. Stimulate Engagement		
	30. Manage Conflict		
	31. Collaborate		
Execution—leaders who deliver exceptional results:			
	32. Focus on Value		
	33. Foster a Climate of Innovation		
	34. Enable Speed and Quality		
	35. Make Great Decisions		
	36. Shape the Culture		
	37. Take Action		
	38. Make the Sacrifice		

Compare your competency scores to the level of importance you rated them. The more important they are and the lower your score, the higher the priority they should be as you continue to focus on your leadership development. Circle the competencies in which you plan to develop further. Number them as priority 1, 2, or 3 as you did in the assessment in chapter 6; or put them in priority order from highest to lowest in importance. Put particular emphasis on the lower-level SCOPE of Leadership competencies in *Self* and *Communications* as they are foundational to most of the higher-level competencies. Build an updated delta roadmap for the most important competency you wish to develop. When you have finished developing that competency and are able to score yourself as a check or plus, go to your next-highest-priority competency. Continue to build and execute an action plan for each competency you need to develop until you have reached the level of competence you need for your leadership situation.

Be patient. Take it one competency at a time. Leadership is a journey, not a destination.

Refer to my book *Activating Your Ambition: A Guide to Coaching the Best Out of Yourself and Others* (www.ActivatingYourAmbition. com) for a straightforward approach to setting goals, building a roadmap of incremental steps, and taking the action you need in order to create new habits, attitudes, and aptitudes. Refer to www. AlpineLink.com and the section on delta roadmaps in chapter 6 for a template to follow in your individual development planning.

Contents of the SCOPE of Leadership Six-Book Series

-Book 1-
Leadership Competencies That Enable Results

Introduction

Chapter 1: The Need to Lead

Chapter 2: Choosing to Lead

Chapter 3: Learning to Lead

Chapter 4: Disruptive Trends Affecting Leadership

Chapter 5: Leadership Competencies

Chapter 6: Building a Leadership Roadmap

Chapter 7: Closing Thoughts

Appendix:

The SCOPE of Leadership Scorecard

Contents of the SCOPE of Leadership Six-Book Series

Figures in the SCOPE of Leadership Six-Book Series

Tables in the SCOPE of Leadership Six-Book Series

About the Author

Books by Mike Hawkins

-Book 2-
Self: Setting the Example

Introduction

Competency 1: Believing with Passion

Competency 2: Pursuing Goals within a Vision

Competency 3: Learning Continuously

Competency 4: Knowing Self

Competency 5: Demonstrating Honorable Character

-BOOK 3-

Communications: Inspiring Performance

-BOOK 4-

Others: Developing People

FIGURES IN THE SCOPE OF LEADERSHIP SIX-BOOK SERIES

-BOOK 1-
Leadership Competencies That Enable Results
Figure 1.1: Skills Versus Sphere of Influence

Figure 1.2: Career and Skill Progression

Figure 1.3: Genetics to Results—Four Levels of Change

Figure 1.4: The Extremes of Competence

Figure 1.5: Leadership Approaches

Figure 1.6: Hierarchy of Needs

Figure 1.7: The SCOPE of Leadership Pyramid

Figure 1.8: Delta Roadmap

-BOOK 2-
Self: Setting the Example
Figure 2.1: Johari's Window

Figure 2.2: Action-Planning Priority Matrix

Figure 2.3: Vision to Execution

Figure 2.4: The Big Picture

Figure 2.5: Workflow Approach

-BOOK 3-
Communications: Inspiring Performance
Figure 3.1: Communications Purpose Matrix

Figure 3.2: Consultative Selling Presentation Flow

Figure 3.3: Communications Framework

Figure 3.4: Five Levels of Conversation

Tables in the SCOPE of Leadership Six-Book Series

-Book 1-
Leadership Competencies That Enable Results

Table 1.1: Measures of Leadership Effectiveness

Table 1.2: Differences Between Leader, Manager, and Individual Contributor Roles

Table 1.3: The Four Stages of Career Contribution

Table 1.4: Leadership Approaches

Table 1.5: Dichotomies That Leaders Balance

Table 1.6: Steps to Running an Effective Team Book Club

Table 1.7: Trends Disrupting the Leadership Status Quo

Table 1.8: Five Capabilities That Determine Athletic Performance

Table 1.9: Considerations in Developing Competency Models

Table 1.10: The SCOPE of Leadership Assessment

Table 1.11: The *Core 25* Attributes

Table 1.12: Factors That Determine Your True Net Worth

Table 1.13: The SCOPE of Leadership Scorecard

-Book 2-
Self: Setting the Example

Table 2.1: Questions a Vision Should Answer

Table 2.2: How to Retain What You Learn

Table 2.3: Tips on Giving Constructive Feedback

Table 2.4: Tips on Receiving Feedback

Table 2.5: Post–360 Assessment Follow-Up

Table 2.6: Nutrition Checklist

-BOOK 3-

Communications: Inspiring Performance

-BOOK 4-

Others: Developing People

-BOOK 5-

Partnerships: Leveraging Teamwork

-BOOK 6-

Execution: Delivering Excellence

ABOUT THE AUTHOR

Mike Hawkins is the award-winning author of *Activating Your Ambition: A Guide to Coaching the Best Out of Yourself and Others* (www.ActivatingYourAmbition.com), a seasoned executive coach, and an expert in improving organizational performance. He is president of Alpine Link Corporation (www.AlpineLink.com), where he is a respected practitioner, speaker, and thought leader on leadership, self-improvement, and business improvement. He is known for consistently leading organizations and individuals to higher levels of achievement.

Prior to founding Alpine Link, Mike developed his practical perspectives on leadership through his unique combination of experience in engineering, sales, and senior management. He has a rare blend of technical, operational, and leadership knowledge. He has worked in multiple industries, including management consulting, information technology, financial services, manufacturing, construction, energy, telecommunications, utilities, and nonprofits.

Throughout Mike's career, he has accepted the toughest assignments and excelled in overcoming the most challenging issues. Few people have practiced, studied, and coached on the topic of leadership to the extent that he has. He truly understands not just what to do and why to do it but how to do it. In his executive coaching experience and in turning around underperforming businesses, he has uncovered recurring root-cause issues that limit performance. As a result, Mike has developed and refined numerous frameworks including the SCOPE of Leadership™, Activating Your Ambition™, and Peak Potential Selling™ to help organizations and individuals break through their limitations and achieve higher levels of success.

To contact Mike Hawkins, e-mail: info@alpinelink.com.

BOOKS BY MIKE HAWKINS

Visit your favorite book retailer or visit www.AlpineLink.com for books by Mike Hawkins published by Brown Books Publishing Group.

Titles include

- *Activating Your Ambition: A Guide to Coaching the Best Out of Yourself and Others*
- *Leadership Competencies That Enable Results*
- *Self: Setting the Example*
- *Communications: Inspiring Performance*
- *Others: Developing People*
- *Partnerships: Leveraging Teamwork*
- *Execution: Delivering Excellence*
- *The SCOPE of Leadership™ Six-Book Series: A Guide to Coaching Leaders to Lead as Coaches*

Help eliminate mediocre leadership.
Learn and apply the thirty-eight competencies of

THE SCOPE OF LEADERSHIP

For additional leadership development resources, tools, and
information, see www.ScopeOfLeadership.com
or contact info@alpinelink.com.